REVISED & EXPANDED

SUDDEN WEALTH...
Blessing *or* Burden?

The Stories of Eight Families & the Financial *AND*
Emotional Challenges They Face with Windfalls

DAVID RUST AND SHANE MOORE

With Psychological Analysis by
Pam Monday, Ph.D., LMFT, LPC and Dianne Arnett, M.A., LMFT, LPC

Copyright © 2013 Clear Standard Publishing, LLC
All rights reserved.

ISBN: 1477512357
ISBN-13: 978-1477512357

DISCLAIMERS

This publication is intended to be an informative and narrative piece outlining key areas of wealth management, specifically related to sudden windfalls. It is not intended to be prescriptive or to imply endorsement of the products, strategies, or processes discussed in the following stories or supporting text.

This publication is designed to provide accurate and authoritative information with the understanding that the publisher is not engaged in rendering legal, accounting, or other professional services. If legal advice or other expert assistance is required, the services of a competent professional should be sought.

DEDICATION

Dedicated to our wives Cyndee Rust and Carol Moore and our children, Kayleigh Rust, and Quinlan and Renny Moore, who have supported our careers, our exodus from the corporate world to become business owners and as authors (for the second time!)

CONTENTS

ACKNOWLEDGMENTS ix

PREFACE xi

INTRODUCTION. xxv

PART 1— STORIES. 1
   Chapter 1: My Rock 3
   Chapter 2: Analysis of *My Rock* 19
   Chapter 3: Gone Fishing. 27
   Chapter 4: Analysis of *Gone Fishing*. 41
   Chapter 5: Looks Like Our Lives
               Are about to Change! 49
   Chapter 6: Analysis of *Looks Like Our Lives*
               Are about to Change!. 65
   Chapter 7: Moving On 75
   Chapter 8: Analysis of *Moving On* 91
   Chapter 9: Happiness in the Rearview Mirror. 99
   Chapter 10: Analysis of *Happiness in*
                the Rearview Mirror 117
   Chapter 11: Roots 125

Chapter 12: Analysis of *Roots*................ 147
Chapter 13: Doctor, Heal Thyself 155
Chapter 14: Analysis of *Doctor, Heal Thyself* 167
Chapter 15: The Sounds of Silence 177
Chapter 16: Analysis of *The Sounds of Silence* 193

PART 2— APPLICATIONS 205
Chapter 17: Building Your Team 207
Chapter 18: Finding Your Team Coordinator........ 235
Chapter 19: Preparing for Your First Meeting....... 261
Chapter 20: Preparing Your Loved Ones........... 273
Chapter 21: A Look Inside Estate Settlement
　　　　　　 and Probate...................... 289

EPILOGUE...............................311
ABOUT THE AUTHORS....................313

ACKNOWLEDGMENTS

We are extremely grateful to everyone who took the time to review our first book on Amazon, send an email, or call with feedback. As we listened to everyone, discussed the topic of Sudden Wealth, either in one-on-one situations or in front of audiences, the human factor or the emotional challenges kept drawing the majority of the questions and curiosity. While everyone appreciates the financial expertise that we bring to the table, we continue to be intrigued with the psychological hurdles of sudden wealth cases. It led us to create the second edition in the series, **Sudden Wealth... Blessing or Burden?**

There are so many professional, experienced, and caring psychotherapists in Austin, but we are especially thankful for our relationship with Pam Monday and Dianne Arnett, who will share their expertise with commentary on each story you are about to read.

We would be remiss if we didn't continue to thank Brad Closson for convincing us that our stories and commentary in sudden wealth cases are worthy of a book or a series of books to help people find clarity when their own sudden wealth situation occurs.

We are thankful to Libby Dawson for bringing her expertise to the Quartz Team and to Jessica Ramirez, the multimedia consultant for our publishing company who was instrumental in the production of this edition.

To our professional partners; those attorneys, CPAs, and bankers who continued to distribute copies of the first book to spread our message, we thank you for sharing our vision of changing the status quo of financial advice.

We continue to thank our wives Cyndee Rust and Carol Moore for never blinking an eye when we say we are writing one book, let alone a second. Their support and increasing involvement in our company is critical to our success.

And of course last but certainly not least, we continue to be humbled by our clients who allow us to guide them toward a healthy financial path.

PREFACE

We have a sign in our office that quotes Ralph Waldo Emerson. It says, "Do not go where the path may lead, go instead where there is no path and leave a trail." This is the type of message that has always guided my life and my career. While Shane and I readily recognize that our corporate backgrounds and training helped form the base for our knowledge and thought patterns, we believe the path we began creating through Quartz Financial over the past five plus years will blaze a positive trail both for our clients and our industry. Twenty-three years of experience tell me that we are on the right path. We believe that we can change the status quo of financial advice and are proud to illustrate our efforts with this second edition in the Sudden Wealth series.

After years of helping sudden wealth recipients, you can't help but be empathetic with the psychological and emotional challenges they are often faced with. From the business owner who sells the company he built, to the son or daughter who handles the inheritance from the death of their parents, to a divorcee coming to grips with new financial responsibilities while grieving the loss of a marriage, these real life situations must be handled both responsibly and with a high level of sensitivity by the financial advisor who is charged with helping them.

Remember that the idea of sudden wealth... or as we define it, "suddenly being responsible for more money than in the past" generates a new wave of responsibilities, or in some cases, newly "recognized" responsibilities for our clients. What typically follows is a certain level of anxiousness or fear. Fear of failure, fear of making wrong decisions, fear of losing money. In my opinion, a financial advisor can hardly call himself "holistic" without understanding and addressing the emotional stress his client may be experiencing. Our partners in psychology have taught us that acknowledging and discussing these issues with our clients will help "normalize the issue" which will lead to an honest and productive dialogue either within their own family or sometimes with the help of an experienced therapist. This dialogue tends to clear the way for the sudden wealth recipient to then be able to make the necessary financial decisions without emotional baggage hindering them.

Rest assured we still follow the principles of financial planning. We believe in creating, executing, and monitoring individual financial plans for every client. We still believe in keeping investment costs as low as possible. We continue to search for strategies that will more fully diversify our client's portfolios. We will always give our cell phone and home numbers to our clients in the event that they have a question after normal business hours. We hope our actions convey the main thing—that we care. We hope that every financial advisor begins to adopt this philosophy.

As with all of our clients, we wish you physical, emotional, and fiscal health.

David Rust

What do we know about sudden wealth now that we didn't know when our first book, *Sudden Wealth... It Happens was released?* Quite a lot actually. Although, wealth management techniques haven't necessarily changed greatly in this short period of time, the book has sparked a significant discussion among different individuals, families, and groups about their financial issues following a life changing event. This is quite a remarkable change. Being a wealth manager since 1994, I can personally attest that people would generally prefer to talk about almost anything before they talk about their struggles with money! Regardless of the conversation, or lack thereof, there are three recurring themes that people tend to come across.

The first, of course, is the psychological impact sudden windfalls can have on individuals and those around them. As conversations with our therapist partners developed, we gathered a tremendous insight into the "whys" and "hows" of sudden wealth recipients' daily challenges and how they've learned to manage the stress.

Secondly, as more and more sources of sudden wealth appear every day we have to continue to field questions about these specific types of sudden wealth events. For instance, Initial Public Offerings seem to be back in vogue with several recent, high-profile IPOs. Energy production and new technologies are spurring pockets of sudden wealth all over the United States. Consolidation in the medical and legal fields is driving more and more business sales. Each of these events instantly creates an abundance of millionaires who may or may not be prepared for the effects of sudden wealth.

And last but not least, we increasingly see evidence that the financial industry's approach to helping sudden wealth recipients needs to be refined. We see examples of wealth managers big and small, from Wall Street to Main Street, focusing a narrow angle lens on their primary area of specialty. Readers have shared stories with us about their "investment guy" suggesting that all can be addressed with their newest product, the "insurance guy" using the same solution for all types of cases, or the "planner" with the big notebook of charts and graphs. Not that any of these alone are bad or unimportant, rather they just don't have a lot of experience from a wide-angle view of all the interrelated issues, financial and emotional, influencing and affecting the sudden wealth recipient's life and decisions. I believe without a high-degree of independence, advisors will continue to struggle finding clarity within the bigger picture.

As the saying goes, "The journey of a thousand miles begins with one step" and, for me, people communicating their financial challenges and opportunities is a tremendous first step. This revised and expanded edition is our next step to further encourage these discussions.

Shane Moore

I started college when I was 17—what does anyone know at 17? Not having a clue of what I wanted to do when I grew up, I took business classes—simply because my mother had a degree in business. I made good grades because I was a good student, but I was so bored! One day I signed up for an elective, a psychology class. And it was so interesting that I immediately changed my major to psychology. It never dawned on me how much schooling I would need to earn a living in that field!

But I had a passion for it! I truly believe it was a calling! People are so complex, and so interesting, and it is a tremendous honor, as well as a huge responsibility, to be invited into people's lives and to hear the intimate details of their struggles. They are trusting me to understand them, and most importantly, to help them. So I continued to learn, receiving advanced degrees, learning and learning all that I could.

But as I learned about psychology—the study of the human mind—I felt that something was missing, somewhere. Much of psychology focuses on the things that are wrong with people. It also often focuses just on one person, and yet that one person interacts with so many other people, especially with their mates, children, and families. I began to notice that people would want to change their behaviors, or their beliefs, or how they thought about life, and yet when they would do something differently, the people around them were often not so happy with their changes! Have you ever experienced that? I sure have! And in fact, mates, as well as folks from the person's family of origin, would especially resist the changes their loved ones made, and would somehow seem to send the message of "change back, change back."

As I was noticing this phenomenon, I began to look at my own family and began to study family systems and the principles of how we are always acting and reacting in patterned ways with the people around us. I discovered in my family that I was the family switchboard person—that meant people would talk to me about the problems they were having with other people in the family, and I would try to help them. And I realized that they were talking about others, rather than talking directly to them. Of course nothing got resolved with the person they were upset about, because the other person never knew about the problem! Oh, they would feel better because I would listen and understand them, but they would not ever work it out with the other person. That's when I began to get it that I needed to do something differently in order to get out of the middle of other people's problems. I began to say "please talk about that problem with Joe" and I would change the subject. That was my change move.

Within two weeks, I started getting calls from my brothers, asking me why I wasn't helping our mother anymore. They were saying "change back, change back." And that really helped me understand that all of us, in our individual "tribes", are so intertwined and the relationships are so very complex. I realized that the way I could help my clients was to help them understand how they and their families were joined together, often unconsciously, in an intricate dance that had the purpose of keeping the family system stabilized. Change coming from one person affected all of the others, much like a hanging mobile bounces around when you pull on one of the parts. As people in my office talked about their struggles, we would work together to develop strategies to change in ways that would help them feel more competent, more confident, more authentic, less depressed or anxious—whatever goals they had. And crucial to this work was predicting and managing how their families would handle the changes, because change is so often so scary. People often prefer the known, even if uncomfortable, to the fear of the unknown. So they began to invite spouses, children, parents, and even grandparents into the office with them so that all could work together to understand each other and support each other as changes were made.

The changes that sudden wealth brings affect everyone in the family, as you will discover when you read this book. Most people don't understand why anyone would be unhappy with getting lots of money! If you are reading this book, then you are probably already facing the challenges that sudden wealth brings. I want to help you understand that the struggles you have are normal! And as you work with financial advisors, insurance folks, lawyers and other professionals, please keep in mind that seeing a systems therapist to learn how to manage the changes that will happen in your family, and with your tribe, is one of the best investments for your future happiness that you can make. Here's to the joy that can be yours!

Pam Monday

My father told me as a young girl that I was lucky to have been born in America, the greatest country in the world; and that I was lucky to have been born in the greatest state in the country (Texans do believe that!) and that I was lucky to have been born into a nice family (and I was). He said, "Now honey, what you do with the rest of your life is up to you."

No matter where we were born or what advantages we may or may not have had we all encounter surprises throughout the journey of life. There are many ups and downs, zigs and zags along the way. Even the most exciting events bring some unexpected challenges. Enduring and surviving the teen years, launching off to college, marriage, the birth of a child, empty nesting, retirement, and ultimately the death of our loved ones present new and unexpected challenges for us all. Sudden wealth brings blessings and burdens, decisions both large and small and certainly some unexpected emotional challenges.

Most often we get through minor and major events just fine and then every once in a while we hit a bump in the road that requires a little extra effort and support. It is important to utilize the tools available to us to manage the challenges that life brings. Family and friends are our first resources and line of defense and can help guide us through uncharted territory. Professionals can supplement that support by helping to decipher some of the issues that arise. I think in our lives there are times we all wished we had reached out a little farther through some troubling times.

Acting as a sounding board and offering a neutral perspective I am honored to accompany my clients as they walk through some of the natural challenges that come with each phase of life. Collaboratively and creatively, as in these reflections we offer the individual, couple or family as a whole stress reduction and problem resolution strategies. A fresh view can bring fresh ideas!

With the words of wisdom from my father, my observations in life and my training as a therapist I have come to understand that each of us enters our position in the world born with a certain personality and disposition formed basically from our DNA composite. The remainder of our personality is formed by our environmental experiences. Culture, family structure, values and beliefs play a big part in those experiences. We look into family patterns that hinder or accentuate positive direction toward the family's goals and how to maintain traditions and rituals or integrate contemporary new ones.

The vignettes in this book depict the stories of 8 families who have experienced such challenges and how they faced, endured or triumphantly navigated them. Their stories parallel typical phases and challenges we may all face though life, and are presented in an entertaining fashion through the lens of these families. As we seek the guidance of a teacher to rear our children or a physical trainer when we strive to reach a new pinnacle of fitness, it is also helpful sometimes to seek the guidance of professional counsel. These families stumbled, were guided into or wished they had met with a financial advisor or counselor after a crisis was thrust upon them. We all have the option of choosing counsel to assist in preventing a problem from developing into a crisis. What turn in the road do you think would make a difference for these families?

The marriage between counseling and financial guidance after the acquisition of sudden wealth is a brilliant union David Rust and Shane Moore have initiated. Our team offers some guidance through these stories as each family encounters likely and unlikely events. Reflectively we ask questions and suggest scenarios to help navigate confidently and peacefully in the management of the twists and turns through the blessings and burdens of sudden wealth.

May your path be abundantly blessed!

Dianne Arnett

INTRODUCTION

In our first book, **Sudden Wealth... It Happens**, we portrayed seven families who received sudden wealth through various life events such as inheritance, divorce, selling a business to name a few. We wanted to illustrate the fact that sudden wealth situations are very common and bring a certain level of challenges both financially and emotionally. We know from experience that the most common initial reaction to the new found wealth is fear. Fear of failing, fear of making a decision, fear of losing all the money. Good financial planning and education can help assuage this fear; provided the sudden wealth recipient isn't overwhelmed by emotions stemming from how the money was acquired.

Since our first book was released, we've found that while many people are definitely interested in the proper ways to handle their sudden wealth financially, the vast majority are also very curious about dealing with the emotional challenges that often accompany the windfall. This interest led us to find psychologists that would have special insight on the topic.

The second edition in the Sudden Wealth series, *Sudden Wealth... Blessing or Burden?* is a compilation of work based on our original seven stories and applications plus a new eighth story. For each case we provide important psychological commentary from recognized psychotherapists Dianne Arnett and Dr. Pam Monday. Finally, given the frequency of cases involving an inheritance, we share insight on what to expect when settling the affairs of a loved one. You'll find this new chapter in the applications section of the book. This book is part of our continuing efforts to educate the general public about the challenges and solutions of dealing with sudden wealth.

About these stories

These eight stories are based on elements of cases we have seen throughout our careers. No one story is about any particular client. There are many different sudden wealth events and certainly hundreds of different outcomes. This book highlights eight stories to illustrate scenarios of sudden wealth that we hope will leave you wondering, "How would I handle the same situation?" Make your own conclusions. Speak with your family members about the stories. You never know, you could find yourself in a similar situation tomorrow. How would you handle it?

PART ONE

STORIES

MY ROCK

"Live as if you were going to die tomorrow.
Learn as if you were going to live forever."

Mahatma Gandhi

Mary and Richard had just celebrated their forty-fifth wedding anniversary. Their children and their families had flown or driven in to celebrate the occasion. Richard was particularly proud on this occasion. Richard and Mary hadn't seen their entire family together in a few years. It again was particularly pleasing to Richard, who had just finished his first marathon with Mary, two of their sons, and three of their seven grandchildren waiting at the finish line. Richard had always been a fit and determined man. As an electrical engineer, he was a voracious reader and had a habit of studying and planning. Much to his wife Mary's chagrin, often his plans were never completed.

The idea of running a marathon was one that had been much discussed over the years but usually not completed, due to family or job responsibilities. Richard had always said that once he retired he would begin his plan to run the marathon. On a Sunday morning, Richard proudly presented to Mary a detailed plan of how he would complete the marathon ten days before his sixty-sixth birthday and two days before their forty-fifth anniversary. He had sixteen months to prepare. He was in good shape. He saw his doctors as recommended. He didn't smoke, didn't drink, and worked out regularly, usually running up to three miles several times per week but never ventured outside the three-mile range.

Mary looked at Richard's highly detailed plan and just smiled. Typical Richard, she thought, always meticulously planning; if only the planning led to completed projects. She began thinking about the unfinished backyard deck, the remodeled bathroom, the plan to finish reading the bible in one year. All of these projects were well planned, but even with the best intentions, they were never completed for one reason or another.

Richard was an excellent husband, but a serious procrastinator in most cases. However, in the weeks and months after his retirement, she had noticed a change in Richard. He seemed to need this race more than his past big projects. She felt a sense of urgency coming from him so she encouraged him more with his running. She learned how to cook specific meals that she read were good for performance or helpful in the body's healing process after a long run. In a way, she learned how to take care of this runner, her husband Richard. Despite being a team throughout their marriage, she was often left out of Richard's big projects. Now she felt like she was an integral part of Team Richard. With his retirement and this latest project, Mary felt closer than ever to him, this made her very happy.

Week after week, Richard continued the process of increasing his endurance while Mary continued operating the "running kitchen." Mary kept a log of the meals he enjoyed and those that were most efficient, depending on what Richard's immediate need was when recovering from a long run or preparing for a long run. Richard wrote a daily running log and kept their family up to date on his training and progress through texts, e-mails, and Facebook. He marveled at how on top of the social media he was at his age. Their granddaughter Cindy even said they were "the coolest grandparents on the planet." This was their ten-year-old granddaughter who thought many things were the coolest things on the planet, so they took the compliment with a grain of salt. Nevertheless, a compliment coming from one of the grandkids was always appreciated.

With a determination Mary had never seen before, Richard accomplished one objective after another, and proudly displayed every checkmark next to every distance he completed right on schedule just as he planned. He was less than two months from accomplishing a goal he had spoken of for years. A goal that quite frankly Mary never thought he would reach. Their Sunday brunch ritual that Richard had suggested fourteen months ago had brought them closer and closer. The thousands of calories he consumed served him well in getting the week off to a good start. Richard was weeks away from running in his first marathon. He was signed up, and two of their children would be there at the finish line. Their oldest, John, would help the family follow Richard's run online.

Mary

I was so proud of the progress Richard was making. I learned how hard it is to prepare for a marathon, and even more so for someone sixty-six years old. Richard was like the mailman. Rain or shine, hot or cold, he was running. He showed a commitment that I had never seen in him, especially for a physical challenge like a marathon. The stronger he grew in determination, the more I wanted to support him. I did my own research and learned the best ways to feed him, to fuel the engine of a runner in training for a marathon. I was so proud of him and so happy to be such a large part of perhaps one of his biggest accomplishments. Still one Sunday morning at brunch, I couldn't help but worry about his health, in particular about a cough he had developed a few days earlier that wasn't going away. I asked him about it, and he shrugged it off as a cold. At the time, the marathon was only a week away, and I couldn't imagine him running that far with a cold or a cough. For Richard, he had come too far, trained too long and too hard, to let a little thing like a cold get in his way. But for me, I still couldn't stop worrying, and I didn't really know why at the time.

It's interesting that Richard finished the marathon the same week as our forty-fifth wedding anniversary. The two milestones have uncanny similarities and we've taken both in stride (pun intended!). The marathon was a tremendous accomplishment for Richard, and I know he is very proud of himself. He finished with a slower time than he wanted, but just to finish his first marathon at sixty-six is something that he is so excited about. He nicknamed himself "Route

66." No one really understood why, but he thought it was cool, so for the weekend of the marathon and our anniversary, everyone called him "Route 66." It was good to see him celebrate his life in that way. It was almost as though he was reborn. The grandkids noticed how much more positive he was at the anniversary party. Several of the kids commented on their father's new outlook on life. We celebrated with our family all weekend, and to me, these were the best of times.

Two weeks later, Richard decided to go for a quick run one morning. A quick run for Richard was most likely a five miler these days, and that would normally take him about an hour. When he called from his cell phone after twenty minutes, I wondered what the heck was so urgent that he would interrupt his run. I teasingly answered, "Route 66 hotline." A woman I didn't know was on Richard's phone. She told me that he had fallen and had asked her to call me before he passed out. She also said that she ended up calling 911 before calling me and that an ambulance was on its way. After a few agonizing minutes, she told me where Richard was going. I rushed to the hospital.

Richard was in the intensive care unit. The doctors told me he had had a major heart attack and might not live through tomorrow. My mind was racing. I needed to call the kids. I needed to see Richard, and he needed to see me strong. Would he be awake? What would I do without him? He makes the big decisions; he is the rock. He is my rock. I can't live without my rock!

Richard and Mary's son Ken

Dad died two hours after arriving at the hospital. Fortunately, I was able to make it to the hospital and see him just before he passed. My mom was in a state of shock, as we all were. We had never seen Dad in such good shape as he was in the past year and especially right up to his running of the marathon. Mom had mentioned that Dad had a cough for a few weeks but had passed it off as heartburn or allergies. That was really the only minor indication that he wasn't in perfect condition for any man, much less a man of his age. I helped Mom with the hospital paperwork and began conversations with the funeral home and their church. I searched through Dad's desk at home to find many papers related to final planning only to realize that nothing had ever actually been decided. Luckily, I did find a term life insurance policy on Dad for $1.5 million, so I felt better that Mom would be okay financially. Amazingly the policy was just three months from expiring. Other than his IRA, of which they were already living off, I found no other assets. Judging from Mom's mental state, I knew that the next few days making these decisions would be excruciating for her and that didn't even include making any financial decisions.

Mary

My mind was in a complete fog. The questions seemed to keep coming at me non-stop. Do you know your husband's social security number? Did your husband wish to be buried or cremated? Do you want a rosary? Will the casket be open? What type of flowers do you want? What kind of thank you cards should we order? The obituary is due tomorrow afternoon; do you have something prepared, or do you want us to write it? I felt like I answered more questions in the twenty-four hours following Richard's death than I had in our entire marriage. Richard always handled the big decisions and even many of the small ones. I was unprepared and, at times, almost ashamed to admit how angry I was at him for leaving me so unprepared! The questions continued: Do you want a reception at the church following the funeral? Are you interested in seeing our tombstones? How many death certificates will you need? Do you want an obituary in any other cities? It was just too much, too much.

Eighteen Months Later

Richard and Mary's Sons: John, Ken, and Jim

John

My mom struggled in the months following our Dad's death. Normally a cheerful woman, she became gloomy and insisted on staying in the house. Many times we tried to take her to dinner or just out for a walk, and she stubbornly resisted. Early on, we tried to talk to her about her finances because we knew Dad used to handle all of that, but she wouldn't talk about it and said she was "handling it."

Ken

We tried to get Mom to visit with a financial planning team that specialized in "sudden wealth" or inheritance cases, but time and time again, she refused and told us not to worry, that Dad had provided well for her. I seriously doubted that whatever she thought she was "handling" that she was doing it correctly.

Jim

Ten months after Dad's death, I flew in from Seattle to visit Mom. I brought my kids thinking that would cheer her up, but on more than one occasion, she would get confused with the kids' names. She was irritable and looked disheveled. Mom was always so meticulous with her clothes and her hair. On this occasion, her clothes looked like they had been worn several days in a row. She had no makeup on, and her hair hadn't been washed in a while. I was scared. I had never seen my mother like this and suspected that she might have had a stroke or was suffering from dementia or Alzheimer's.

When she decided to take a nap, I started looking through papers in my dad's office. I was shocked to find that she had made large donations to several nonprofit organizations, had bought penny stocks, and three time-shares, to name a few of her financial transactions. I knew that Dad had a life insurance policy for $1.5 million so I was further alarmed when looking at her bank account: my mom had only $947,000 left in her account. She had gone through $553,000 in less than a year. I called my brothers.

John, on behalf of the family

Six months after Jim's discoveries, we were finally able to get my mother in an assisted living arrangement. Six months had passed because it took us that long to convince her. We tried reasoning with her, telling her she could pick the best place for her needs.

We told her she would make new friends and that she would be safe. Nothing was getting through to her, and we became increasingly concerned that she could hurt herself if she stayed at home alone any longer. After several more attempts, we convinced her that this was "Dad's plan" all along. We told her that Dad had planned for them to live in a particular home and was going to surprise her at the right time. We hated lying to her like that, but it worked. We got her moved in and we felt some relief that Mom was "safe." The doctors told us that her Alzheimer's was advancing quickly and warned us that at sometime in the near future, she may not recognize any of us. We felt we were running out of time. Through the legal process, we became responsible for Mom's finances. She continues to fade from us, a little further each time we see her. I'm shocked to think that less than two years ago, my Dad had run a marathon and my parents were the happiest people in the world, celebrating forty-five years together. Now Dad is gone, and while Mom's body is still with us, her mind steadily retreats from us. She has deteriorated so quickly.

Authors' comments

This story may seem dramatic, but it happens every day. Whether the wife or the husband, the family "rock" tends to take on too much of the financial responsibilities without the knowledge of or the input from the other. Rarely will this person seek guidance or advice from financial professionals. The spouse of a "rock" often has no interest at all in learning more about their financial health. When something happens to the "rock", the other is left hopelessly searching for answers.

Although this story illustrated the quick decline of a surviving spouse, frequently the surviving spouse can live in good health for twenty to thirty years after the passing of their loved one. For that reason, a comprehensive financial plan is necessary to ensure that the surviving spouse will not "outlive" their wealth. Long-term care coverage should be part of the plan in the majority of cases. Most people do not realize that the average annual cost of staying in a nursing home is over $75,000 per year[1].

---

1   Genworth Financial, "Genworth 2010 Cost of Care Survey" (2010).

The elderly are also preyed upon by criminals of all types via the telephone and e-mail. Without a financial support team, the wealth of the remaining spouse could disappear quickly.

One final thought for "the rock" in your family. Is your spouse prepared to handle the financial responsibility of sudden wealth as a result of your death?

> I hold it true, whate'er befall;
> I feel it when I sorrow most;
> Tis better to have loved and lost
> Than never to have loved at all
> ***Alfred Lord Tennyson***

ANALYSIS OF *MY ROCK*

by Pam Monday, Ph.D., LMFT, LPC

Oh sudden death! It is not meant to be. It is out of sequence. It is devastating for family and loved ones. I know that pain personally, because my own father died in a boating accident. My mother was left with plenty of money, but she too felt Daddy was her "rock", and she had to learn how to handle all of the finances, and take on all of the responsibilities that she had never had to deal with. Let's talk about death and dying, something we usually avoid talking about.

All of us have difficulties dealing with aging. All of us have difficulty thinking about death, even if we have strong spiritual beliefs. Many of us avoid talking about painful things, not wanting to upset others or ourselves. We avoid talking about change, such as how our lives will change when we retire, or what would happen if one of us dies. We avoid even thinking about these painful things, and thus of course avoid taking steps that would help ourselves and our family members deal with life when the event happens. We stay in denial, our heads in the sand like ostriches, and then disaster strikes. Sudden death is so overwhelming to families that if we do not get help to deal with the enormous emotional upheaval it creates, then family members begin to get symptoms that signal the emotional pain. Mary was so overwhelmed, both by her grief and her total dependence on Richard to take care of her in every way, that she not only got depressed, but began a rapid decline into dementia. Other ways that symptoms show up in families dealing with sudden death include someone beginning to abuse drugs or alcohol; someone's marriage dissolving; kids acting up and getting in trouble—these things and more are signals that people are hurting, and need to talk about what they have lost, and how they can help each other heal from the pain.

My own family experienced many of these issues after Daddy died. How I wish we had gone to family therapy sooner than we did. Not wanting to increase others' pain, we each grieved alone, and pretended everything was fine when it wasn't. Some of us immersed ourselves in work; others put on a false front of functioning to the world only to secretly disintegrate into the inability to get out of bed when home, alone and lonely. A teenager began to do drugs and act up, which served the purpose of diverting attention from our overwhelming sadness when we had to focus on helping the teen. But that was just a distraction. The sadness, the powerlessness, the anger, the guilt of being the ones to survive, the inability to think straight, the difficulty functioning from day-to-day—these things always came back when the immediate crisis with the teen passed. When we finally went to family therapy, we felt immediate relief, not only to begin to open up about all those feelings, but also were able to reconnect to each other, supporting each other and helping each other find solutions to the problems the sudden death had created.

If you have experienced sudden death, and have struggled with any of these feelings, I urge you to find a competent therapist who specializes in dealing with grief. The enormous changes in every area of life that accompany sudden death experiences are overwhelming to all. You can't even begin to focus on managing the sudden wealth that death may have brought if you don't first deal with the grief! A spouse who is totally dependent on the other spouse feels terrified and totally inadequate, unable to figure out on their own what to do without the constant guidance the spouse provided. Wives need to talk about all of the fears they have, and sort out all of the conflicting emotions they are experiencing. They will then be able to get clearer about what to do next, and how to use resources to help them learn the things they need to learn to function better, one step at a time.

Adult children need to get help to know how to deal with their own grief, as well as how best to support and help their remaining parent. Grandchildren need help understanding what has happened in the family and how to deal with their pain and confusion. Often children keep feelings inside, not wanting to bother the parent whom they see having a hard time because of the death. They begin to feel responsible for protecting the parent, and end up not getting what they need to feel better. This can create academic, social and emotional problems that don't go away with time. Families can learn in family therapy how to have these conversations with each other, and how to be open to listening to each other's pains. Paradoxically perhaps, sharing pain does not increase the pain; instead, it speeds up the healing process.

No one can predict sudden death. But if you and your spouse have the kind of traditional relationship that Mary and Richard had, then it would be a great idea to go to a therapist soon and talk about your fears. The husband could talk about the responsibility he feels to protect his wife from worry, and how important it is to his self esteem to be both protector and provider. The wife could talk about how she avoids talking about things that might make her or her husband anxious or upset. She might talk about her sense of inadequacy about financial issues, or making decisions, or being in charge.

They could talk about what they each learned in their families-of-origin about how to deal with problems, or how not to deal with problems. Are they doing what their families did to avoid dealing with problems? Were problems discussed openly in their homes? Who in the family handled the finances? Did their parents have traditional marriages, and if so, how did their parents handle aging, death and dying? How did people cope with stressful events, or transitions and change? The therapist could help both of them look at what they might do differently now, so that they could feel better about facing retirement years together, or aging together, or facing the inevitability of death that always comes, sudden or not. They could make a plan about how they would deal with each life-changing event. They could make a plan about how to organize and then share information with their adult children so that the kids could know how to handle things if one or both of them died suddenly.

These are the kinds of conversations that a therapist can help you have. A good therapist can help people stay calm so you can talk about these things without a lot of reactivity. You can learn how to strategize and make plans and feel confident that your family will be able to manage the challenges that aging and dying inevitably bring. And most of all, you will feel a sense of empowerment, a strengthened emotional connection with your family, and the peace and relief that comes from knowing you have done the best you can do to help your family, in life and through the pain of losing loved ones.

GONE FISHING

"We have it in our power to start
the world all over again."

Ronald Reagan

James had been looking forward to this day for years. He had worked in various positions of authority for years at the same company and its subsidiaries. His company went through several buyouts and in the long term he was rewarded generously. Working in a time when companies matched generously at 5 percent in his

401(k), his loyalty and tenure, he believed, would provide a sense of long-term financial security for himself and his wife and hopefully add financial flexibility for his children and grandchildren.

In spite of the financial perks his company provided, James spent many days at work thinking about anything but the work. His job as a research scientist had become monotonous and unchallenging years ago, and he was counting the days until he could retire. Twenty-eight years of "the career" was wearing on him. Two years prior to the actual retirement date, his company offered a generous severance for early retirement, and he jumped on it. His wait was over. All those years of building his wealth and, in a few weeks, he would become a millionaire. He would have over $2 million—an amount of wealth that would now carry him and his wife for the rest of their lives. It was an exciting time. He kept thinking to himself, I'm going to be a millionaire! He was fifty-nine years old, and his new life was right around the corner. After a retirement party, where he would be given the customary wrist watch in front of his family, co-workers, and friends, James would finally get off the treadmill called "the career". In one week the only business card he would carry would read, "James Snow, Ph.D, happily retired". In one week, he could buy a boat. In one week, he could go fishing anytime he wanted. This was an especially funny thought, since he had never been fishing and the idea of fishing had never interested him much, but when you're retired you can do whatever you want, whenever you want, he thought.

James

I had known for years how much my 401(k) and pension plan had grown over the years, so the possibility of retiring early couldn't come too soon. I saw the numbers every month, but it never really hit me until I rolled it into an IRA and the term millionaire came to mind. I was proud of myself for all that I had accomplished and was so excited about retiring early and being able to spend more time with my family especially on the family boat that I was about to buy! My wife Ann and I would begin traveling to see our kids and grandkids.

The idea of not having to get up early everyone morning and drag myself to work, of being able to enjoy a great cup of coffee (especially after I started cultivating my own beans!), read the paper slowly, and figure out my day was making me giddy just thinking about it. And to think that I get this new life, and I don't have to worry about money anymore, makes us feel extremely fortunate and blessed.

Ann

James has been talking about retirement for what seems like the last ten years. We've talked about how we will spend our time together, and we had decided that buying a boat would be a good way to spend more time with each other and our entire family. James has been doing his research, as he always does, and he found a beautiful boat that can hold up to fifteen people, so we're very excited about having the first of many family reunions on the lake. I am going to keep working at the library for a few more years, which should help with our transition, so we aren't bumping into each other after he retires.

I enjoy my job, so I have no plans to retire soon, and I think James is very happy with that as well. We feel so blessed to be in a position of not having to worry about money.

James

We rolled my funds into an IRA with a national brokerage firm. It was certainly a reputable firm and didn't charge us any fees, as I understood it. We moved the money into an IRA and pretty much mirrored the same types of investments that I had been using in my 401(k) plan at work. Being fifty-nine, I felt I still had plenty of years, so I could afford to be aggressive with our money in the hopes that it would grow even larger. From time to time, my guy would call me with a couple of investment ideas, but for the most part, the transition of the money was very easy. I could make withdrawals over the phone directly to a checking account, so that was very convenient too.

We decided that we would like to pay for our six grandchildren's college education, so we knew that there would be future expenses we needed to cover, but we felt that with an average annual growth of 8 to 10 percent, based on the historical averages we had been showed, we would easily be able to help our kids with those costs. We had a small mortgage that we refinanced to a very low rate, around 5 percent. We didn't hold any debt, and besides buying the boat and remodeling the house, the grandchildren's college tuition would be our largest expense for a while in our retirement years. I felt it was important to share our good fortune with our kids and grandkids. We made the commitment to use our money to help create family memories (hence the beautiful boat that I bought!) and to enhance their education. We felt that was a more appropriate and thoughtful way to share our wealth with our family rather than shower lavish gifts on them every year.

Three Years Later
James

How's retirement going? Well, I thought the last thing I would be doing is worrying about money and it seems like that's all I do with my "spare time."

Things went great that first year! We traveled to Europe, bought a boat, had a family reunion, and remodeled the house. Our investments held up pretty well. I think we earned close to 6 percent that year. Retirement was everything I thought it would be and wanted it to be. "Not a care in the world," I would tell people when they asked me about retirement. Life was definitely good!

But little did I know that problems in the economy were brewing. I didn't do any fishing those first three years, but financially speaking, I feel like I've been swimming in rough waters for some time now, and I'm tired!

The second year, the markets went crazy, and we had banking panics. The result—my IRA dropped 39 percent! During all of this, I called my guy several times, and he advised me each time to stay put. He reminded me of past crisis and how the markets always rebounded. He told me to hold on and everything would be just fine. Before I retired, I rarely watched CNBC or any other financial networks and rarely read the Wall Street Journal or other publications of that kind. But during that second year, it occupied my time almost night and day. I've heard since then the comment "Don't be a prisoner to your wealth." That's exactly what I had become, a prisoner! I was a prisoner to listening to and reading about the latest bad financial news of the day. Not that I could do anything about it. Day after day, it was bad news. There was talk of a recession or was it a depression? The government was stepping in to save banks and large insurance companies. With no financial background myself, I just kept reading more and more and watching more and more of the financial news. I would call my broker over and over, and his message never once changed. He would always say, "Yes this is a bad period, but we've been through bad periods before and always come out of them." I asked him, "What do I do if this time we don't come out of it?" He answered, "We will." I shot back, "When?"

Ann

We are trying to remain positive in spite of the financial difficulties of the last three years. We were able to do some wonderful things once James retired, but since the economic downturn, our life has gotten a little out of control. I certainly was planning to work a few more years, but my position at the library was eliminated about a year after James retired. We've always lived comfortably and rarely worried about money. James earned a good salary at his company, and my job at the library allowed us to spend money on vacations and gifts. We never lived extravagantly, so money wasn't usually a topic of discussion for us. James has never been one to watch the stock market or read financial publications, but for the past two years, he seems almost obsessed with it. I know he's worried about things, even though we still have plenty of money, still over a million dollars; but I know it's much less than we expected to have after only three years; and at this point in our lives, he worries whether it will be enough, especially since we're still paying for our grandkids' college. At this point in our lives, I worry too.

James

After hearing the same story from my broker time and time again, I decided to tell him to just sell everything and go to cash. At least that stopped the bleeding. By the time all was said and done, one day I had almost $2 million, and the day he sold everything, we had $1,197,328.12. Oh yes, I remember that number to the penny.

How in the world could something like this happen? I blamed my broker. I blamed myself. I blamed the president, the government, the greed of big corporations. It seemed that I had enough blame to go around, but in the end, it was my money, and I was making the decisions. I must have made the error. I was making the decisions…I was making the decisions! Anyone hearing this story must wonder why I was the one making decisions, a research scientist with little financial background. I consider myself a smart guy; I do have a Ph.D. But in reality I don't have a clue when or what or how to invest money. It looks so much easier than it actually is. I need someone who is experienced with these matters, and someone I can trust to put my interests first. I don't have the slightest idea where to start, all I know is that the advice I've gotten so far hasn't worked.

One Year Later
James

I could have kept my money in cash as I had done for almost a year now, but I knew that wasn't really a strategy at all. I was frozen, and I was scared. I just didn't know what to do and didn't know whom to trust.

So I went back to my roots—I did research. I spent the next few months just talking to friends, former colleagues, and people at church. I did research on the different specialties and found what type of advisor I might need. I learned about the many different designations that advisors/planners hold. I learned the different ways they are compensated. I actually learned the difference between captive agents and independent advisors operating as a Registered Investment Advisor (RIA) or through independent broker dealer channels. I asked many people many questions.

I did my homework and found two firms that I thought would fit the bill. Both firms were similar, both independent without corporate agendas (that was an important aspect for me and Ann!) with backgrounds in money management, financial planning, and insurance strategies. We did a thorough interview of both and checked three references on each firm. Both firms were excellent. We would have done well with either firm, but we thought long and hard about it, made our decision, and haven't looked back.

By the time the new firm was handling our money, it was definitely less than what I had started out with, but because they constructed a plan to meet our needs, we feel confident that our goals will be met. We have long-term care insurance now on each of us in the event that we need home care or, heaven forbid, end up in a nursing home. We can rest easy knowing that we won't be a financial drag on our children.

We still will help pay for college tuition for our grandkids, albeit with a few tighter parameters, like only four years at a state school, but we feel good about that. We still spend time with the family on the boat like before. Our vacations may end up being less frequent and mainly in the United States, but hey, there is so much to see in our great country that we still feel very fortunate that we can experience it, sometimes even with the kids and grandkids.

Hey and I've even taken up fishing!

Authors' comments

Frequently the soon to be and newly retired get caught up in their new lives, especially how they will spend their recreation time. If the retirement amount they receive seems large enough at first glance, they buy cars, boats, make financial promises, and plan large vacations. Without an initial financial plan specifically mapping out their wants and needs, it is easy to overlook the ramifications of the timing of returns.

It is common for investors, and sometimes their advisors, to extrapolate the historical average annual returns as a static return that reoccurs year after year without fail. In the case of the Snows, they and their first advisor failed to realize that negative returns, particularly large early on can do substantial harm to the long-term success of their retirement plan. A more conservative approach to their portfolio would have been a more appropriate approach and could have saved them thousands of dollars in losses.

The Snows eventually learned the hard way that all advisors are not created equally. They have different backgrounds, specialties, and experience. The Snows realized that they were working with a broker who was merely executing orders that were deemed suitable. James also acknowledged that he himself wasn't qualified to manage his own money. They also learned how difficult it is to manage money, particularly when the economy and the markets are in a tailspin for one reason or another.

This story turned out well because Mr. Snow was smart to realize that he was in over his head and smart enough to finally do the research to find the firm that would help him spend more time fishing instead of worrying.

> "The trouble with retirement is you never get a day off."
>
> *Abe Lemons*

ANALYSIS OF *GONE FISHING*

by Dianne Arnett, M.A., LMFT, LPC

Fishing, playing with the grandchildren, remodeling the house or building the dream house, getting fit, reading all the books that have stacked up on the nightstand, or sipping margaritas on the beach... Retirement, like sudden wealth, immediately conjures up images of freedom, relaxation and unlimited opportunities with family and friends, hobbies, pursuits and the joy it all brings! Whether spending more time with old hobbies or launching a new adventure, the opportunities are endless. Retirement can be all of those things and more. It is a time in life like no other. When people retire they have flexibility in their schedules as in their youth, yet the wisdom of a lifetime. It is a great time of life!

Most couples coming up on retirement plan long term for the big event and are caught off-guard by the magnitude of change. James and Ann were no different. A shift in a couple's relationship and lives together begins before retirement arrives as they visualize their new roles. Dramatic life-changing events can bring unexpected surprises, as other milestone phases in life, like the introduction into college, graduation, marriage, the birth of a child, empty nesting and grandparenthood. Each phase brings some unexpected surprises that no amount of planning will prepare you for. It is sometimes difficult for well educated and competent people to realize that they need a little help from other professionals. As in James' professional and personal life, others sought him out for advice and consultation. It is common for the family provider to be unaccustomed to being on the receiving end of help after a lifetime of leadership responsibilities. If it hadn't been for the down turn in the economy, this couple may have postponed seeking help and things may have declined to an unsalvageable point. Oh, what a difference a phone call can make! What is true in the financial advisor's office is also true in my office. I have learned that the sooner the phone call is made when a problem arises, the better for those involved, And that is a good thing!

I encourage my clients to, "Make a plan and be flexible," no matter what phase of life they are in when they come to see me. The planning part comes more naturally for some and the flexibility part comes more naturally for others. I often find both exist in a couple and sometimes neither! Many of the retired couples that I work with come in after they have begun the financial planning because that process revealed the need to look at the other elements of their relationship. Most couples do well in the first months after they retire because they have had a long list of things they wanted to do when they, "finally had the time." Struggling with a new routine after the initial big projects or trips have been made is common. Even though married many years most couples have spent their days apart until retirement and can find themselves reporting to their friends and family that their spouse is, "getting on my nerves." In therapy we look to see if the annoyances are truly new or perhaps behaviors that have always been there, but ignored over the years filled with demanding schedules. Planning out new specific daily schedules and the big special events go a long way to reduce tension. Having a therapist, like a good financial planner, who can direct the conversation can really be beneficial and avoid some unnecessary strain.

Long-term married couples who have figured out their problems together over a lifetime, or ignored them until one of them "gave in," sometimes have a more difficult time seeking out counseling. Adult children are often the catalyst to therapy as they notice the growing tension between their parents and encourage them to make an appointment. Usually the children do the research and give them my name and number. Often I see several generations in the same family. My 35 year old client, Sarah, persuaded her folks to come in by simply asking them, "It is only an hour of your life; what do you have to lose?" The idea of therapy sounded foreign to her parents when initially suggested, but became a little easier for them to accept when Sarah shared that in the previous year she and her husband had used therapy to get them over a rough spot. People who have never experienced counseling, especially couples in their late 60's or 70's, often believe it is only for the seriously mentally ill or couples on the verge of divorce. During the introductory session they quickly learn that it isn't like the scene from an old movie where they lie on the couch for a five-year stint of psychoanalysis!

A brief introduction explaining what therapy is all about is given to the individual or couple who are first-timers in the therapist's office. I always have them fill out a brief historical profile and sign a consent form to treatment. The consent forms indicate fees, available appointment schedules and the reassurance of confidentiality. It does not contain a long-term commitment for an unending amount of therapy sessions! In fact, I always ask my clients to explain their current problems, any changes they would like to make and what it will look like when we are finished. Their description is a good place to start the conversation and helps me to judge when we can wrap up therapy. People like to know that therapy has a beginning, middle and especially an end! James and Ann, like many couples, may have been surprised how friendly and easy conversation flows between themselves and the therapist.

Any nervous feelings are quickly dispelled as the details of their concerns are approached. Some of the disagreements may be as common as division of duties such as who will walk the dog, do the shopping, laundry and cooking, or cleaning the new boat! Laughter ensues and collaboratively, we discuss the issues common or uncommon to retirement. Every phase in life includes growing pains. Redesigning days, filtering through the priorities each have on their "bucket list", finding new purpose in life outside their careers and relationship, goal setting with realistic expectations and understanding of one another's hopes, needs and dreams are some of the many topics we talk through. I validate that frustrations that arise through the adjustment phase are natural and very common. I may suggest joining a class, activity or senior group, as meeting with others who have experienced and conquered similar new challenges offers new insight and broader perspective. A professional who has counseled with such persons can likewise be helpful or even enlightening. James and Ann may have experienced a gentler transition into their first few years of retirement if they had made calls seeking both financial and emotional guidance early into their retirement. Any new experience is eased with support from friends, family and a few experienced professionals. Couples have reported that working as a team has made things a little simpler and more manageable.

Unlike friends and family who may have a personal agenda, a therapist who possesses experience in dealing with issues that arise surrounding retirement can lift some of the pressure off the couple and ultimately the entire extended family. Therapy can also ease the pain of delicate discussions surrounding end-of-life decisions. Compassionate conversations stimulated during therapy sessions prior to dire circumstances reduce stress in the future for the spouse and children at moments of extreme emotion. It is common for my clients to return for sessions to address a new challenge or tweak the plans we previously made together.

No one approach to retirement works for every individual, couple or family. Some people easily move through notable transitional phases while others find such transitions frightening, uncomfortable and unsettling. The goal is to retire successfully in all areas of life. Retirement, like the other monumental phases and challenges, requires evaluation, experimentation and reevaluation. Your path will be the right one for you, your spouse and your family if you are true to yourself and those closest to you. It's a fabulous new phase in the journey through life! Retirement presents opportunity! How will you make this time of life an abundant blessing?

LOOKS LIKE OUR LIVES ARE ABOUT TO CHANGE!

"The only way not to think about money is to have a great deal of it."

Anonymous

The Hamiltons were like most typical middle-class American families. They were in their early forties with two children, ages fourteen and ten. Chad was a fireman, and his wife Susan worked in administration for a hospital. Their lives frequently revolved around the activities of their kids. Driving their children to and from band practices and soccer and practices and games ruled their time most days in a week. With combined salaries over $80,000, the Hamiltons were not by any definition wealthy, but they lived comfortably and within their means. Different from many of their friends, they were dreamers and had a running dialogue about how they would spend their lottery winnings.

Not only would they talk about how they would spend their lives in luxury once "the big one" hit, but they also actually bought lottery tickets every week. Every week Chad would buy $5 worth at a gas station near the firehouse, and Susan would buy $5 worth at a convenience store close to the hospital on the south side of town. At $10 a week, $40 a month, $480 per year for fifteen years, they executed this futile exercise in "wealth development." The consistency with which they executed this plan might seem a little crazy to some, but for the Hamiltons, it was fun to dream, especially when according to them, "it won't pay if you don't play." Their friends teased them with all sorts of pet names, like "lotto losers," "best friends of the Lottery Commission," "money burners," and so on. Chad and Susan shrugged it off and jokingly told their friends that when they hit the big one, none of them would be invited on the cruise vacation they would be hosting for only their favorite people. To them, playing the lottery was fun. Discounting Chad's weekly poker game and an annual trip to Las Vegas during which they only gambled with a predetermined amount of money, they oddly never considered themselves gamblers, per se.

Susan liked to buy books on architecture, mentally planning the mansion they would build if they ever hit the big one. She enjoyed watching shows about the lives of the rich and famous. She read magazines on luxurious vacation spots around the globe. When prodded about her fantasy life, she was known to smile and say, "A girl can dream, can't she?"

Sometimes they did wonder if they were a little crazy, especially when they accounted for all the time and money involved in this "plan" to create wealth. In fact, the thousands of dollars they had already spent playing the lottery seemed as though it was more destroying than creating the wealth they hoped to gain from a lottery windfall.

Their financial situation took a serious hit when Susan lost her job unexpectedly. Now with a keen eye on every dollar going in and out of their household, the "lottery dream" was in jeopardy of losing its weekly funding. Although it was only $10 a week, they began to look at this futile exercise as a waste of money at a time when they could least afford to be wasteful.

Susan

Since I lost my job, I've really been trying to be smart with our money. I've cut back on our spending on clothes and at the grocery store, and we're eating out much less. I'm even considering canceling our little weekly "lottery dream." I mentioned it to Chad, and he just said, "It's only ten dollars a week Susan!" Well, I added up how much we've spent on the lottery all these years, and it came to over $7,000 dollars! I had no idea we had spent that much, and considering all of the other financial responsibilities we have, I feel pretty stupid. And I have no idea how much Chad spends on his weekly poker game. We could really use $7,000 right now!

Chad

I know Susan is worried about money since she lost her job, but really, $10 a week isn't going to make us that much better financially. Besides, if we quit playing the lottery, it is guaranteed that we won't win. The dreams we've shared every time we play are fun. Sure it costs a little, but what if we were to win? Then it would all be worth it, so I plan to keep on playing.

The Hamiltons continued to struggle financially until Susan found a job four months later. The new job paid her almost as much as her old job, but Susan continued her frugal ways and stopped buying weekly lottery tickets. Knowing this, Chad took it upon himself to double the amount of money he was spending on the lottery each week. Most weeks he would take the money out of his "poker winnings."

Two Years Later

Checking his lottery numbers early one morning while Susan was still asleep, Chad let out a scream that woke up the entire family.

Chad

Susan had stopped playing a couple of years ago, but she didn't know that I had been playing for her. We hadn't really talked about it in a long time. The morning we won was so surreal. I always checked my numbers online and lately had been doing that early in the morning either at the station or in my man cave at home. We had won small amounts before, $100 here and there, but never once had we come close to hitting all of the numbers.

I couldn't believe my eyes when the first three numbers matched, and then with my heart pounding, verified that every single number matched. We had just won $14 million! I ran around the house screaming, "We won; we won; we won!" and banging on doors. Susan was in a state of shock, and the kids were jumping around screaming, "We're rich; we're rich!" We called my parents and Susan's parents. In an hour, our house was filled with the entire family. We made a big pancake breakfast. We sat there all morning and talked about all the things we could do with the money. Everyone chimed in with the excitement of the next idea. Things just couldn't get any better. It was a great day.

We decided to take the upfront payout over the lifetime payment as we had always said we would do. The lump sum ended up being about $8 million after taxes, which still was a very large amount of money.

We got online to plan the cruise we always said we would take if we ever hit the big one. We spent the entire day looking at cruise dates, and figuring out who we would take with us. By the end of the day, we had chosen a seven day cruise to Alaska and our guest list was fifty-two people! We spent the rest of the evening on the phone making our invites.

Looking back on this day, I can't help but think that planning a cruise should have probably been way down on the priority list of to-do's, but we were just so excited that we wanted to share with all of our family and friends!

Our list of invitees to the cruise grew larger as more of our friends and family found out how much we had won. On the day of the cruise, I had a list of invites in my hand that totaled seventy-two people! But hey, we had won $8 million, so we could afford to treat everyone and were happy to do it!

Three Months Later

By the time the cruise was over, we were definitely in need of a vacation! We now had to find a lawyer to help us with the legal aspects of winning the lottery. We used a lawyer that several of my buddies knew from the station. He was a divorce attorney, but said that most of the documents he would draw up were boilerplate and that he could handle those. We opened three bank accounts and were, of course, treated like royalty. We had never really had money outside of our 401(k) plans in the past, so we didn't have a financial advisor, and I kept getting mixed advice on who to turn to. I decided to table the decision in spite of countless phone calls and letters from financial advisors, financial planners, insurance agents, you name it. It was like our contact information had become worldwide knowledge and everyone knew that we were lottery winners. We changed our phone number to an unlisted number, but somehow we continued to be peppered with people trying to help us invest our winnings.

Susan quit her job and spent most of those early days looking at pictures, architectural plans, and interviewing builders for our new home. She was determined to build our dream house, and it, along with the kids' activities, occupied all of her time. For me, I decided to stay on with the fire department, at least until the end of the year.

Susan

We feel very blessed that we won the money, allowing me to quit my job and spend more time with the kids. Planning and creating a dream home consumed a lot of time as well, between meetings with architects, designers, and builders.

We had a great time on the cruise, except it was pretty disappointing that no one offered to pay for anything the entire time. We never really said, but we thought we were just paying for everyone's cruise. It turned out we paid for everything from pictures to bar tabs to excursions. The amount was already at over $120,000, which is a lot of money. I felt a little bit taken advantage of when no one offered to help with any of their expenses incurred on the cruise. But as Chad said, "None of our guests had just won eight million dollars, so we were happy to do it". Of course, we were happy to do it, but still, I felt a little bit used.

Thirty Months after Winning the Lottery
Susan

Most people would not believe me if I told them the last two and a half years have been more like a nightmare for our family. Most people would think I'm crazy that I'm complaining about the life that comes with being a lottery winner. I'm pretty much shocked myself. I've lost friends, who have called me a snob to my face, the same friends that we've taken on vacation and paid for the entire thing. My kids have been teased about being rich. My extended family is constantly asking for money for one thing or another, and Chad's family hasn't been much better. Chad said he could manage the money, but he has clearly been out of his element, which has been the primary source of our arguments. Plus, he spends at least once a month in Las Vegas playing poker. I feel so isolated from everyone. I told Chad we need professional help for our marriage and our finances to help us cope with all of the other situations that being lottery winners brings.

Chad

I'm sitting here today with almost $3 million in the bank, and I feel like I've been through the wringer. I feel like our marriage is on the rocks. Seems like all we've done for three years is argue about money. I think we did some things right, but clearly we did more things wrong and it has taken a toll. We've been seeing a marriage therapist for the past two weeks at Susan's insistence. Our therapist says that we're not unique in letting this type of wealth dictate actions and to become somewhat lost in it all. We didn't set out to mismanage the whole situation, but clearly, we never had a plan from the beginning, and it (the money) has just run our entire lives.

I just remember reading so much negative press about the financial industry, and I thought I (we) would be so much better off if I was in charge of managing the money. Obviously I don't have enough background or education to do a solid job, and many of the investments I chose have lost a lot of money. Susan has clearly lost faith in me, and in that regard, I don't blame her. On the other hand, she has done a great job, if you think spending a lot of money is a great job!

Three Months Later

The Hamiltons showed up for an appointment with a wealth-management firm that specializes in sudden wealth cases. The firm was recommended by their psychologist. Beaten down by the entire experience of being lottery winners, they are ready to listen to advice.

Authors' comments

Chad and Susan ended up finally getting the financial advice and guidance they needed from the very beginning. They were advised to build a spending plan. They were assisted with finding a CPA and a board-certified estate-planning attorney, which were necessary as part of the Hamiltons' new financial team. They were guided in identifying what they truly needed in their lives versus what they wanted. This helped them create and understand their future financial road map. The oversight of their investments was turned over to the new firm. Knowing that the Hamiltons had just lost a substantial sum of money in their most recent investments and were extremely risk averse, a conservative game plan was devised for the short term until they could gain confidence in a more typical risk/return model for their needs and age. They were advised to purchase umbrella insurance, which would insure them against lawsuits above and beyond the typical coverage they were carrying. Their life insurance needs were reviewed. They agreed to sell their home (valued at $1.5 million) in order to downsize to a more modest home in the $500,000 price range.

Chad and Susan

Clearly we feel blessed by the lottery winnings, and we did a poor job of being good stewards of the money. It almost wrecked our family, but we're determined to keep this good fortune to help us create a more positive environment for our family and those who love us. We trust our financial advisors and our therapist. They have clearly done this before and understand our needs and challenges. We feel so much better knowing that we now have a plan and a team of professionals who are going to help us follow it. Life is definitely better with a plan.

> "Alas! Old man, we're wealthy now,
> It's sad beyond a doubt;
> We cannot dodge prosperity,
> Success has found us out.
> Your eye is very dull and drear,
> My brow is creased with care,

LOOKS LIKE OUR LIVES ARE ABOUT TO CHANGE!

> We realize how hard it is
> to be a millionaire."
> *Robert W. Service*
> *"The Joy of Being Poor"*

ANALYSIS OF *LOOKS LIKE OUR LIVES ARE ABOUT TO CHANGE!*

by Dianne Arnett, M.A., LMFT, LPC

Winning the lottery is like getting on a roller coaster! You're excited you are taking the ride, but there are so many unexpected twists and turns and it is a relief when the ride levels out! Chad and Susan ultimately found their way in and out of lottery winning highs and lows. Hindsight is always

20-20 as we look at our past decisions. Being overwhelmed with excitement and acting impulsively cost this family a great deal. I wonder what their first year would have looked like if they had slowed down and sought professional advice the week they matched those magical numbers. If you ever find yourself in unfamiliar territory it will be the day you win the lottery!

As the authors, Rust and Moore, mention you will need to talk to bankers, lawyers and financial advisors to help manage the money. Chad and Susan were surprised to find themselves in a counselor's office as well. Most men think, "I wouldn't be caught dead in a therapist's office." Men like to please their wives and often come to therapy for that reason alone. It is a good reason and gets the ball rolling toward a new perspective. I find most men dread it when their wives make that first appointment, but are happy once they come! Wives and children are happy too! Usually, as in Chad and Susan's story, the wife (or mother) makes the phone calls. Women reach out to friends and family with problems, sometimes just to vent their frustrations. Receiving and deciphering conflicting advice can be confusing. Women will be more likely to ask for directions on a trip and more likely to ask for directions through emotional challenges. In general, women are more comfortable openly sharing their stories than men. Women like to solve problems through talking and men like to solve problems through action. Both can be accomplished through therapy! Chad was feeling as if he was losing his family and when he considered therapy as part of his plan of action to pull his family together it made sense to him. Men have been taught, directly and indirectly, their entire lives to be strong and protect their families. Chad, like many men, may have felt it was part of his duty to protect when he agreed to go with Susan for counseling. In therapy, practical plans of action are established. Goal setting is an important part of the first session in therapy. Men especially find concrete goal setting in therapy surprising and appreciate the direct approach. It gives them a plan and specific things to do after they leave the counselor's office. After the first session the mystery of therapy is removed and everyone is comfortable. This is when the work in therapy begins.

That work consists of opening up and talking about family values, decision-making strategies and setting boundaries. As in Chad and Susan's case, we might start with their first big lottery decision and how it leads to the cruise debacle. The unexpected charges for extras and hurt feelings created by friends and family would be deciphered. We would look at how Chad and Susan as a couple have made decisions in the past. Couples are encouraged to talk about what has worked in their marriage and what hasn't. Recalling decision-making successes is a good place to start in therapy. Focusing on the positive sets a good mood for compromise and change. Identifying success in other areas of their lives can help the couple to apply similar approaches to the decisions that need to be made around the lottery. It's funny how the venues change, but couples seem to stumble through problems the same way over and over throughout marriage until finally seeing the repetitive patterns. This happens even with couples in long-term marriages!

Chad and Susan got swept up in the excitement and let others direct their decisions. I wonder if that is a pattern that they have experienced in other areas of their lives. It may be common for them to act spontaneously, which works well in some circumstances, but causes problems in others. Opposites attract! It is common in a couple for one spouse to act more spontaneously and the other to be a planner. Identifying differing behavioral patterns create "Aha!" moments and help establish new patterns for the future. New approaches require sacrifice and compromise on both sides, but are so much easier to put into action once common pitfalls are clear to both husband and wife. Establishing guidelines quickly after their winning ticket was discovered could have reduced Chad and Susan's stress early on and prevented many of the problems and losses they encountered. This is a great example of that 20-20-hindsight enlightenment!

We all find ourselves in new circumstances throughout our lives and seeking the help of professionals with emotional objectivity can help ground a family during stressful times. A therapist's role is to be certain that each participant gets an opportunity to express their opinions and then to follow up with questions that lead toward compromise and problem resolution. I have adopted a strategic step-by-step process to look at possible options for problem solving that I teach my clients. This methodical approach aids a couple or family to approach their problems in a collaborative, controlled manner. They can apply it to any conflict that arises in the future. It has been enormously successful!

Family values, patterns, respect and closeness cover a broad spectrum and will play a big part in how conflicts are handled. As all couples, Chad and Susan grew up in different style homes with different values on parenting, social responsibility and money management. Coming to therapy can help a couple to identify the past differences, strengths and weaknesses and how they play a role in their current decisions. Some of the hurt feelings they were experiencing over the lottery decisions are most likely similar to past hurts. Old issues seem to surface at this stage in the process. In such cases the therapist helps the couple to reinterpret or redirect and stay on topic. During therapy we collaborate to create a practical plan of action for each element of the winnings that must be dealt with by the individual, couple and family as a whole. Financial investments and strategies are turned over to our financial advisors, Shane and David. Each spouse contributes and I will help them sort through the obstacles that arise. Typically, they will feel better in just a few sessions. Making decisions becomes easier when a concrete plan is established and ultimately, fewer arguments arise.

Lottery winners almost always receive financial requests from family, friends and non-profit organizations. It can be overwhelming for a family who has acquired sudden wealth to navigate through the requests. Your financial advisors will be helpful in the money management, of course, but dealing with the guilt that comes with having to say "No" can be painful. In therapy, we address the issue of guilt, develop boundaries and discuss how to manage the conversations. Together we set out a course of action that is comfortable for everyone. We even role-play such conversations in the office. I'll set up the scenario to be enacted, typically using one of the encounters the family has experienced. These role-plays seem a little awkward at first, but quickly laughter breaks out, roles are exaggerated, some steam gets let off and all those participating get into it! It ends up being a fun activity and one of the most practical tools of therapy. Role-plays help everyone feel better equipped to handle the next request.

Issues that impact one family member impact every family member. In the case of a family who wins the lottery, I would invite the children to come in as well to discuss the impact all of the change is having on them. Unexpected concerns are often uncovered when the children come into session. It is not uncommon for them to share comments that have been made to them by their peers. It is fairly common for children whose parents have won the lottery to be teased, even harassed! We brainstorm on ways to manage negative interactions in the future and help them find the words that will be effective with their friends and classmates. It is common to see children become reclusive from their friends or act out if they are being teased. This can have an enormous impact on their social interactions and happiness. We've all experienced teasing in our childhoods and it is a relief to children to have the support of family to deal with it. Giving the children direction offers a huge amount of relief and comfort to them.

The children are included in making some of the decisions. The children will have opinions about things that impact them directly and things that don't. They definitely have ideas about how the money should be spent. Putting an X-Box in every room in the house was a suggestion of one 10 year-old boy! Of course, not all of their "brilliant ideas" are incorporated in the family plans, but they feel part of the process and it brings the family closer together. Most families soundly agree they wished they had come into therapy sooner.

Universally, what I have found in all families who have come into unexpected wealth is to take things slowly and resist making any fundamental changes abruptly. When a family treats themselves to some things they have needed and they could not afford before the windfall they get to scratch that itch to spend. They make bigger changes gradually and do all right. Think it through, talk it over with a friend or family member and then finally with a group of professionals you trust who have no emotional or financial stake in your decisions. Being deliberate and working collaboratively helped Chad and Susan after attending a few therapy sessions. Integrating children into the process brings the family together sometimes in ways they have never encountered before. It certainly shows the children that it is a good thing to reach out for help when you need it! They can apply what they learn in session to family meetings at home. Chad probably admitted therapy wasn't what he expected, it wasn't scary at all, and he was grateful it helped, It helped his family reconnect with one another and reestablished their true values. The lottery winnings were not as important as keeping his family together and happy. Going slow will decrease the chances of getting into more than you bargained for and will increase the chances of long-term peace and happiness. This approach will seem less like a roller coaster and more like the steady pleasant ride of a merry-go-round!

MOVING ON

"Life's challenges are not supposed to paralyze you; they're supposed to help you discover who you are."

Bernice Johnson Reagon

Natalie Jentz's mother, Rose, was eighty-one years old when she died. Rose had been diagnosed with breast cancer at seventy-three and had fought her way to being cancer free for five years, until she relapsed fourteen months prior to her passing.

During that time, Natalie, her only child, was her primary caregiver, her cheerleader, her best friend. Rose spent the last few weeks of her life in hospice care two blocks from their home, and if Rose was awake, Natalie was usually there by her side.

Natalie's father had died eight years earlier. His death was sudden, and it had hit Natalie hard. She vowed afterward to spend as much time with her mother as possible, even more so when Rose's cancer reappeared. Prior to her dad's death, she and her mom hadn't been particularly close. She had always been a "daddy's girl." But since her dad's passing, Natalie and Rose grew to understand each other, and in the end, they were the best of friends.

Natalie

My mom was so picky about her hair and her nails that I always had to make sure they were done just right. She ended up needing a wig, because she said that many of her friends, "the ones that were still alive," might not have seen her in a while, and since this was the very last time they would see her, she had to look her best. So I made it happen, and Mom looked just beautiful.

At the service, the church was full of people and the reception was "exactly as we had discussed." Mom wanted the reception after the funeral to be uplifting so we had music playing. Mom and I chose all of the songs and put them on an iPod. During her last few days, the music played in her room nonstop. Everyone who visited her just danced into her room. Even when she was in so much pain and slept most of the time, she seemed to be smiling because of the music. I had a video created using pictures of her life that was set to her favorite songs. I didn't finish it until the day before she died. I tried to show it to her, but she wasn't awake to see it. I regret that, because I know Mom would have loved seeing the final product.

There's still so much to do. I need to get over to her house and clean it. Eventually, I'll need to interview real estate agents, but I don't see any urgency there. It was Mom and Dad's house for thirty years, so I figure it will take a lot of time to clean it and sort through all of the memories before I sell it. There's no harm in being diligent. I'm sure it's what mom would have wanted. Mom's dog, Max, is with us and finding his way just fine with all of us. The kids love having him around, and I'm sure Mom is happy knowing that Max is happy. That reminds me, I will need to change his vet soon. All in good time.

Randy (Natalie's husband)

I'm worried about my wife. Natalie's devotion to her mom's care these last few years has been admirable, but I wonder if she will be able to find balance again. She hasn't spent much time with the kids or her friends over the last year. She didn't cry at the funeral and seems to be in an almost "robotic" state. She was busy planning the funeral and the reception and making sure the kids had the right clothes to wear. I know that everyone deals with grief in different ways; I understand that; I'm a teacher, not a psychologist, but I do understand the grieving process. Natalie seems to be a little too much under control right now. Even when our youngest, Emily was crying at the reception, Natalie acted as if she didn't have time for her. I'm concerned and hope this will get better over time.

Six Months Later
Natalie

I really miss my mom. We had grown so close over the last few years. I shared everything with her and we of course would talk or see each other every day. I feel like I'm missing an arm or something.

I've been very busy settling her estate, getting her house ready to sell and things like that. I know that she would want the house in tip top shape before we put it on the market, so I've done some things like installed hard wood floors, got it repainted, and finished the garage floor so far. There's a ton of landscaping work to do still, so I spend a great deal of my day at her house overseeing the work.

Randy thinks it's a waste of time and money, but he isn't as attached to the home as I am, and I'm using some of the inheritance money to do the work, so it's not like the remodeling project is coming out of our checkbook. Plus, the girls can come over here after school to do their homework at the dining room table, just like I used to, while I'm supervising the work. It's not like I'm neglecting them. Both of Randy's parents are still alive, so he doesn't understand how important it is to do this the right way. I keep telling him, this is what mom would want and he says that's my answer to everything lately. I think he's overreacting and in reality wants me to spend some of the inheritance money on a boat or a new car, something for him. Settling an estate is a process, and he just doesn't understand any of it. Hopefully he'll learn from this experience because his parents are in their late seventies and won't live forever. We didn't have a lot of money before Mom's death, so it wouldn't be right to just start spending her life's savings. It wouldn't be right to suddenly change our lifestyle because my mom died. It seems so disrespectful to start spending her money and just sell her house for whatever we could get because we didn't take the time to get it in perfect shape. I'm not doing anything differently than Mom would do if she were alive. I think it's what any good daughter or son would do.

Ten Months after Rose's Death
Natalie

We've made great progress on Mom's home, and it should be ready to go on the market as soon as I find a realtor. I'll start interviewing realtors next week. The house ended up needing a new roof. Well, it didn't have to have a new roof, but it was sixteen years old and looked worn to me, so I got estimates from a few roofing companies and got the best bid. They just finished the work, and it looks great. My mom would be thrilled. Randy is constantly losing his patience with me every single time I spend any money on this house. It feels like he just wants it sold and out of his life. I refuse to short change this. I am representing my parents and I'm convinced they would think I am doing this the right way. So far I've only spent around $50,000 getting their house in order, and I'm positive we'll get that back through the sale.

Randy

I hate to say this, but I thought we would actually find some peace after Natalie's mom died.

It was such a struggle for Natalie during her mom's last few months, and I really thought that while she would be very upset at her mom's passing, she would eventually heal, settle the estate, and be able to benefit from the inheritance that her parents left her.

The past year, yes, her mom is gone, but Natalie has engrossed herself in her mom's affairs. I understand that she needs to sell the home, but she has almost practically remodeled the entire home! It's not even the money that bothers me; it's the amount of time she has spent getting the house ready for sale. I mean, it's been almost a year now, and she is just now working on interviewing realtors. She hasn't begun looking at all the stocks she inherited, and I'm afraid there's just one project after another right around the corner. After the sale of the house and all of the stock, we (she) should have around $1 million. Certainly that's a significant amount of money for our family, but we haven't seen any of that money yet because Natalie can't seem to move on.

Eighteen Months after Rose's Death
Natalie

I closed on Mom's house today. We didn't get the price we were asking for, but pretty close. Randy will most likely remind me that we didn't get back the $50,000 we put into it, but at least it sold in three months, so that's good. It feels so strange, no longer being responsible for my parents' house. They had lived there for so long. I did everything I could to get it looking like I think they would have wanted it to look before turning it over to another family. My dad didn't like spending money on things like remodeling, but I know that Mom would have wanted the house fixed up before selling. So I'm comfortable with everything we did to sell the house.

Randy should be thrilled because we just got $378,000 wired into our account today. That should keep him quiet about how much time I've spent settling Mom's affairs, though we still need to talk to someone about all the stocks she owns. I don't really know any stockbrokers, so I'll need to do some research on that and wrap my head around the whole investment thing.

Randy

I am relieved and, yes, happy that at least this part of settling Natalie's mom's estate is over. We will really be able to use the money. To think that we can fully fund our kids' college with some of this money is huge! Paying for college won't be an issue for us now, and I'm extremely thankful to Nat's parents. They also have almost $600,000 in a few stocks as well. If it were me, I would just sell it all and move on. I just want my wife back. Our girls want their mother back! Natalie's been so consumed, first with taking care of her mom while she was ill, then getting her house ready to sell, and now whatever she's planning on doing with the stock that was left to her.

We need to find a financial person to help us, but I don't dare mention that to Natalie for fear that it will start yet another time-consuming project to work on. I still worry about her, because in my layman's opinion, she hasn't dealt with her grief. True, she is handling things, but the "things" seem to be taking far longer than they should.

Twenty-three Months after Rose's Death
Natalie

I'm so upset. I've been interviewing financial planners, wealth managers, and investment advisors lately. I can't believe there are so many different titles for these people! It's hard to tell the difference between all of them. But the firm I spoke to today really upset me. The people said that the firm specializes in sudden wealth cases and that an estate of this size and simplicity should have been completed months ago. He recommended a psychologist the firm works with in order to help me deal with my grief. They said therapy is common in these types of cases to help those left behind move on. I suggested to them that they don't understand what it's like to lose a parent, much less both of them in such a short time. One of them said he had lost both of his parents recently, but still, that doesn't mean I didn't handle Mom's estate properly. I was thorough, and I continue to be thorough, to handle things the way she would have wanted.

I couldn't believe that I was sitting in a financial advisor's office, and he's recommending I see a shrink! I just broke down crying and told Randy we needed to leave.

Randy

I'm pretty sure that Natalie broke down because she knew that those guys were simply being honest with her. They obviously have done this many times before, and they were simply trying to help her. I think it hit home with her. Besides me, nobody else has told her to move on. Nobody else has told her that things were taking too long to settle. Nobody else has told her that she was filling her days with her parents' affairs in order to avoid admitting that they were both gone. She got in the car and just bawled. I held her for what seemed like forever. She cried two years of tears, tears that I always thought I would see but never did. For the first time in almost three years, I felt I had my wife back.

Twenty-six Months after Rose's Death
Natalie

I'm in a good place now, I am. That day in our financial advisors office just hit me like a ton of bricks. At the time I didn't understand why something two complete strangers said would upset me so much. I got in the car and couldn't stop crying and shaking. Randy was very patient; he just held me and said everything would be okay. Those words were some of the last words my mother said to me before she died.

The financial advisors were right. I had been holding on to my mom by not settling her estate. I kept myself busy, I ignored my kids, and I shut out my husband. Unconsciously, I put them through the hell I was feeling. I've been in therapy, and I feel so much better. Yes, my parents are gone. They were wonderful people and great parents. I'm so lucky to be their child, and I will always carry them with me.

But as for the living, I'm a mom again, and I'm a wife again. I'm moving on. I'm finally moving on.

Randy

We actually hired the financial group that upset Nat. They were experienced in planning, investments, and insurance, and they were frank and honest as well. They dared to risk losing us as clients by being straight with Natalie. We might still be interviewing advisors if they hadn't help break through the wall that Natalie had built over the last few years. I appreciate them so much for helping my wife move on. We now get to move on as a family. I know that's what Nat's mom would have really wanted.

Authors' comments:

The emotional aspects of inheritance can often leave the inheritor stuck: stuck in unspoken emotions, stuck in the logistics of settling the estate, or stuck in any behavior that keeps the inheritor from moving forward. Often, the inheritor feels guilt about benefiting financially from the death of a parent or loved one. A spouse who feels his or her partner is moving too slowly to find closure can exacerbate this guilt, and it can cause serious stress in the marriage. Some inheritors can also exhibit a strong tendency to seek their parents' approval "from the grave." This tendency can leave them almost frozen to making any decisions on the inherited investment portfolio remaining, especially in the case of stocks or land their parents might have owned for years.

It helps for inheritors, like Natalie, to work with wealth managers who are well versed in sudden wealth cases. The emotional aspects of inheritance can never be overlooked. An experienced advisor who can be compassionate but straightforward can usually help break the barriers that exist due to the death of a parent, spouse, or partner.

It is also helpful to seek psychological counsel because the relationship between fiscal and emotional health are so intertwined. In the case of inheritance, robust mental health is a necessary and powerful resource to becoming a fiscally healthy inheritor. When inheritors are focused on the present, they can focus their mind and energy on the creation of the financial plan appropriate to their new level of wealth.

> "We all at certain times in our lives find ourselves broken. True strength is found in picking up the pieces."
>
> *Jill Pendle*

ANALYSIS OF *MOVING ON*

by Pam Monday, Ph.D., LMFT, LPC

Most of us understand that the death of a spouse is one of the hardest things to imagine, but many of us don't realize that the death of a parent will impact us in ways we can't even fathom. If both our parents are dead, then the impact is even more profound. When our parents die, we all have to face our own mortality, and that can be frightening indeed. And when a parent dies, we are faced with all of the unfinished business, and the unresolved feelings, we may have had with them. But it can also be a wakeup call to make our own lives and our relationships the best that they can be, because we truly begin to get it that life is so very short.

Natalie was an only child, and that is at once a blessing and a curse when facing our parents' deaths. She was the sole heir, but also the only person who had to bear the burden of responsibility of handling all of the countless details that need to be addressed after death. Siblings can pull together and help each other emotionally as well as divide up the responsibilities, both before and after the death. But the task of an "only" is much more complex and emotionally heavy. There is no one to share the memories of a lifetime with these parents, and no one to share the complex emotions of preparing for a parent's death. Because she had experienced the sudden death of her dad, she and her mother could be more prepared for death by planning for the funeral and talking about death openly. That makes things so much easier.

But Natalie did what so many of my clients have done when facing their parents' death: they focused intensely on spending great amounts of time and energy on their parent, but disconnecting from their spouse, children and friends.

That is so very understandable, isn't it? After all, we can't be in two places at once, and we can have compassion as someone does all they can do to spend quality time with a beloved parent who is dying. We don't want to be selfish or demanding that the person be there for us. But how long do we have to wait? What are the long-term consequences to the neglected marriage or the neglected children or even the neglected friends, when we are preoccupied with the dying person? It is very hard for the spouse not to feel resentment when their own needs are ignored for a long time. And children often begin to have problems in school or at home if a parent is not emotionally available to help them with their needs.

It is significant that Natalie felt mom was a best friend. Significant especially since during her life with her parents, she was not very close to mom, and was "daddy's little girl." She had a second chance with her mother, something that might not have happened if mom had died first! Most of us don't get this chance. And that is where therapy can really help, while our parents are alive! You see, if we have not been very close to a parent, or if we are angry and resentful toward them, or feel betrayed or hurt or abandoned, or have any other unresolved issues with a parent, then while they are dying, and after their death, we will still have unresolved issues with them! And that takes a tremendous amount of emotional energy.

When we are emotional, we are operating out of a different part of our brain than when we are functioning from the cognitive, rational part of our brain.

We are unable to make decisions as well, and unable to prioritize and plan in an efficient manner. Emotion is clouding our judgment! That was what was happening when Natalie was so focused on making the house perfect, trying to anticipate what her mother would have wanted, still trying to please her, and thus still staying intensely, intimately connected with her mother. Consequently, she continued to discount or ignore her children's needs and her husband's needs, as well as his helpful suggestions for things that would benefit their lives in the present. She rationalized her choices, but those rationalizations only helped her feel better about how long it was taking for her to finish the tasks. She was unaware of what she was doing, which is what happens when we are motivated by unconscious emotions.

I have clients who come to talk to me about the guilt they feel that they haven't been able to be close to their parents; or their despair that they can't ever seem to please a parent; or their sadness that their parent doesn't really know who they are. They want to know how to change these things, and I am able to help them strategize and plan for how to address these issues before the parent dies. And we talk about how to manage their other relationships—with spouse, children and other friends—in ways that help them feel connected, even when preoccupied with the emotional pain of facing a parent's death.

I see many couples who have not gotten therapy until they begin to wrestle with the aftermath of the death of a spouse's parent. The longer the dying process or the longer it takes to settle the estate, the greater the possibility for deterioration of the marital bond. Even if the spouse is extra patient, understanding, and compassionate as their spouse's parent is dying, inevitably there is resentment and distancing if they feel there is not sufficient connection or attention to the marital relationship. Getting marital therapy when the spouse begins to feel resentment is the absolute best timing for preventing marital disruption or problems with children who are neglected. I call this "upriver prevention rather than downriver cleanup"! I teach couples how to talk and listen to each other's pain, and how to repair the disruption of connection when the adult child is torn between their relationship with their parents, and their relationships with their own families.

A very poignant part of Natalie's story is when she finally begins to feel again, and she is able, at last, to cry. Her emotional shutdown after her mother died—the shock and denial, the "robotic phase"—is a normal part of the grief process. It keeps at bay the feelings of sadness and loss that can overwhelm the griever. But staying so busy that we never face our feelings keeps us from moving on! When the financial team confronted her with her procrastination, they did her a tremendous favor! Their words broke through her protective defense of denying feelings, and finally, finally—she was able to cry. Only then could her husband reach out and help her, by holding her and telling her "everything will be okay." The message was "you are not alone; I am here with you," and that begins to help her heal and get back to living in the present. If you are facing the death of a parent, or have had struggles since a parent died, come to therapy—resolve those family-of-origin issues, repair your marriage, and discover that you can feel joy again. You will be able to enjoy the legacy of wealth that a parent has left you, and you can pass it on to the next generation.

HAPPINESS IN THE REARVIEW MIRROR

"You gain strength, courage and confidence by every experience by which you really stop to look fear in the face. You're able to say to yourself, I lived through this horror. I can take the next thing that comes along."

Eleanor Roosevelt

People tend to take the little things in life for granted: getting in and out of a hot shower in the morning, getting in the car and driving to work every day, holding on to our kids bicycles as we run next to them the first time they ride without the training wheels. Most of us have never had to look in a mirror and ask ourselves "what will I do now?"

The myriad of things he could no longer do raced through Hank's mind as he heard the doctor say, "Complete T-seven para," defining him as a paraplegic, meaning he would most likely never get out of a wheelchair, never walk again. His wife, Tracey, by his side as she had been since the accident two days earlier, kept reassuring him that he would be okay, that they would work it out. An electrician, Hank wondered if he would ever work again, so how were things going to be "worked out"? His mind raced with questions: "What am I going to do for money?"; "Why did this happen to me?"; "How am I going to be a father to my little boy?" and "How can I ask Tracey to take care of me every day?"

Tracey

I had just picked up our son Zach from day care when my cell phone rang. With a three-year-old in the backseat, I never use my phone when I'm driving. It's a rule that we decided to follow when Zach was born, and we both have always followed it. I had a strange feeling I needed to take the call, so we pulled into a McDonald's to get Zach a hamburger. The man on the other end of the phone was a policeman, and he told me that Hank had been in an accident. I was ten minutes away from the hospital, and it seemed like it took us forever to get there. My mind was racing, and I was so scared. I had a sick feeling that it was bad. I called my mom and Hank's parents. I tried to stay calm because I didn't want to scare Zach. One of the nurses took him to a waiting room where he could eat his hamburger. I told him that daddy had a cut and the doctors were fixing it. I had no idea what I was about to see.

Hank was unconscious, and the doctors were concerned about his back. They were doing X-rays and told me they thought that he may have fractured his back. He had tubes going in and out of him, and he was on oxygen. He was beaten up, with cuts on his face and arms. As if all this wasn't bad enough, the doctor said he might be paralyzed. I couldn't believe

I was hearing that word: paralysis. Hank was a big guy. He had played football in high school and had always been athletic. He was like Superman to me and Zach. He just couldn't be hurt that way.

Looking at him, he looked every bit like a man who had just been broadsided by a delivery truck. He was going through an intersection when the truck driver ran a red light and plowed into him. The other driver wasn't seriously injured, but they did tell me he was apparently texting. Knowing how we both felt about using the phone while driving, I immediately became angry and hoped that the other driver was around so I could kill him! My husband was lying in bed fighting for his life and may never walk again, all because some "moron" had to answer a stupid text! The next forty-eight hours seemed like an eternity. I've never prayed so hard in my life. I made all kinds of deals with God while I waited for Hank to wake up.

He opened his eyes sixty hours after he had been admitted. I was relieved to see him awake and alert but was afraid to see his reaction to the word paralysis. It nearly broke me to see his expression when he heard the news. I knew our lives would never be the same.

Six Weeks after the Accident

Hank's entire family and all of his friends anxiously awaited his return home on a Saturday morning in April. Through the help of his friends in the homebuilding world, they renovated his house for wheelchair accessibility. Because they lived in a one-story home, they didn't have to install elevators or lifts of any kind. His band of brothers had spent the last couple of weeks renovating the home. Though they still felt awkward around Hank and didn't quite know what to say to him in the hospital, renovating the house was something they could and wanted to do for Hank. The weather that morning was cool and the sun was shining. Unfortunately Hank's mood didn't match the weather.

Tracey

The six weeks in the hospital were challenging for Hank, to put it mildly. He continues to hope that he will walk again, and anything less than that is unacceptable for him. I admire his determination, and I realize there are medical advances all the time with spinal cord injuries, but I'm afraid that if he ever lost the hope of walking again, it might destroy him. He's always been a big, physical man, and if you take that away from him, I don't know if he can recover from that. He was happy to be home, but you could see it in his face that he didn't like the attention from something like this. Put thousands of people around Hank watching him play football, and he would eat that up. Here he was at home, surrounded by those closest to him, and all he wanted was to be left alone.

Hank

I'm happy to be home, I am, but I'm tired of people telling me to stay positive and treating me differently. I'm twenty-eight years old. I almost feel like I'm dead, and I'm the only person that knows it. My focus is to walk again. Anything short of that is failure, and failure is not an option. I appreciate everything the guys did to make it easier for me to use the wheelchair in the house, but in reality, I'm just not planning to need this wheelchair long term.

Five Months after the Accident
Tracey

I feel like I'm always using the word challenge. Our life is a challenge. Hank faces daily challenges. When people ask me how he's doing, I just say it's been a challenge. Hank feels his next challenge is to walk, and while I still admire his determination, the goal of walking again is a huge challenge. I need to stay positive and supportive, as his mood is quick to anger these days. It seems like his frustration grows every day. We haven't seen any progress that will lead to walking and when he is frustrated, he takes it out on me. I'm hanging in there, but it's a "challenge."

Authors' Comments:

According to a study by the Dana and Christopher Reeve Foundation, there are approximately 6 million people in the United States living with paralysis[2]. The challenges these individuals and their families face can be daunting. To the uneducated eye,

---

[2] Christopher and Dana Reeve Foundation, "One Degree of Separation: Paralysis and Spinal Cord Injury in the United States" (Short Hills, NJ: 2009).

the only challenge a paraplegic may face deals with is the obvious lack of ability to stand and walk. In reality, paraplegics face other medical challenges related to blood clots, pneumonia, skin sores, bladder infections, and depression, to name a few. The financial cost is estimated from $681,000 to over $3 million for a twenty five year old person. To learn more about the challenges of paralysis, see www.christopherreeve.org.

Eight months after the accident
Tracey

We're doing okay. I've changed my "go-to sentence" these days. I used to talk about our challenges, and now I just tell everyone we're doing okay. I need to stay positive for everyone especially since we've seen no progress on the stand and walk front. Hank is still determined to walk, but he seems to be at least accepting the fact that for now, he needs to function as well as possible from his chair. He has hired a junior electrician to help out on new construction, as it's typically difficult to gain wheelchair access to a home in the construction phase. That is a big improvement and makes him feel better that he is contributing to our finances again. The medical bills have been large, but thank goodness, we have health insurance through my company, or I don't know what we would have done. Hank's parents helped us buy a vehicle constructed for wheelchair accessibility which allowed him to drive once he got his "sitting license." He wouldn't admit it, but getting the sitting license gave him a boost. It made him feel like a man again. It's only been a few months, but he is slowly gaining back some of his independence. He's becoming quite proficient in maneuvering his chair, but downplays that. He still views his chair as his "temporary means of transportation."

We finally got around to meeting with an attorney that specializes in truck accidents. He seems like a nice man and says we have a great case, but told us to prepare for a long fight. The settlement could be large, but Hank is only twenty-eight years old, so comparatively speaking, the financial challenges of his paralysis over the course of his life will undoubtedly be large as well.

Hank

I hate to say I'm doing better, because, well, I'm still in a wheelchair. I am working and driving, so I guess its okay to say I'm at least getting around better. I guess I still have my good days and my bad days. There are many things to cope with every day, and I'm learning that every challenge I face whether it's a big one or a little one won't kill me and will most likely make me a better person. I've accomplished things I never thought I could do early on after the accident. I'm learning that I can be a man, a husband, a father, and an electrician just like I always was. No, I'm still not walking, but as Tracey reminds me all the time, I'm still here, alive and functioning. I still want to walk again, and I'm hoping that through the help of my lawyer, we'll eventually gain some type of settlement to help with my recovery and future costs. I'm not going to count on a settlement, but given the size of money my attorney says he will fight for, I can't help but imagine what life would be like with a few dollars in the bank. My hope is that a settlement could at least make life easier on Tracey. This has been tough on her and my little boy, and even though the accident wasn't my fault, I still feel guilty that she has to do so much for me every day.

Eighteen months after the accident
Hank

I've learned over the past few months that life definitely doesn't stop for the disabled. I see things differently now. I don't have to work; I'm able to work. I don't assume I'm a good husband; I work hard at being one. My relationship with my son is like healing waters for my body, mind, and soul. He's taught me about unconditional love. He reminds me that no matter what physical challenges I have, I am and will always be his dad. He's five years old now and getting to be such a big boy. We play football on the living room floor. He does all the running and I do all the tackling. He loves it, and so do I. I've taught him to fish. We go to ball games. We do the things that fathers and sons do. Life is still life, and I thank God I'm alive.

Tracey's life is closer to normal again. There were times in the past few months when I couldn't imagine how she was coping with it all. She was filling the roles of mom, dad, nurse, wife, and head of household while holding down a full-time job. She has had some bad days, sure, she's only human; but her positive spirit and her ability to handle the challenges of the day continue to feed my drive and my energy. My life used to revolve around my paralysis. Now with her continued presence and support, my heart is full. I can still be a good man, husband, and father.

Tracey

I'm so proud of Hank. I never thought you could take something like walking and running from Hank and have him deal with it so well. I underestimated my husband. He had a few shaky months where he was discouraged, but who wouldn't be? The mental aspects of paralysis are almost more to bear with than the physical. We used to worry about things, like how he would do his job or even take care of Zach when I wasn't around. We've all just adapted. I love watching him play with Zach. They are two peas in a pod. Zach is daddy's little man like always. Our marriage has survived and even gotten stronger through all this. We even went on a date last week! Hank's right in that life doesn't stop just because you have a physical challenge. We handle the challenges in front of us, one at a time, and in spite of some pretty big challenges, we're doing just fine.

We are waiting, somewhat anxiously, for news on the lawsuit. Our attorney tells us we should receive anywhere between $4 million and $8 million. I can't even imagine that much money. If it happens, we will definitely find someone to help us manage it. Hank has been doing some research on financial people just in case the news on the settlement is good. Neither of us has a financial background, and we may need all of that money to take care of Hank over the years so we have to be smart about it.

Twenty-six Months after the Accident
Tracey

The settlement will pay in about a month. It's just unbelievable. We're going to receive $3.6 million after attorney fees. With everything we've been through, it's almost like justice will finally be served. The money won't make Hank walk again, but hopefully it will provide for any future issues he may have, and it should give us more options financially.

Hank

This settlement is huge! Over $3 million, that's a lot of money! You bet I would give it all back to walk again. The price of not standing or walking is a lot higher than $3 million, I can tell you that. The past couple of years have not been easy at all and the daily challenges now and in the future could sink many people. But we decided months ago that we wouldn't let this beat us, and it hasn't. So we'll take the money, and I promise we'll make smart decisions with it.

I've had a lot of time to think about this and I think I know what I want to do. Everything I've read says I'm going to need a few people to help us manage this money. My list so far has a financial planner, CPA, an estate attorney, an insurance agent, an investment advisor, a property and casualty company, and a long-term care company. I don't have the time, nor the inclination, to know how and where to find all these people. I'm going to look for someone who can play the role of my quarterback. Then I'll have the quarterback find and coordinate the rest of my financial team. That's my goal, so that's what I'm going to do.

Authors' comments

Hank and Tracey found their quarterback. They found a firm that functions as sudden wealth strategists. Hank and Tracey's sudden wealth strategist has many functions, but one of the strategist's primary functions is to coordinate the many advisors they will need. Obviously every sudden wealth recipient is different, but generally a person will require a team of advisors with special experience and specific knowledge in various fields. Some sudden wealth recipients may already have part of their team in place, but many come into sudden wealth needing the entire team assembled.

Some of these specialties include professionals who understand and advise on the complexities of tax and estate planning, not to mention the myriad of insurance strategies and products combined with the overall creation of the financial plan and investment plan, their execution, and the monitoring of their performances.

Often including a psychologist as part of this team proves beneficial. The events leading up to a sudden wealth event may be traumatic and require a few sessions with a psychologist who understands the entire emotional spectrum of sudden wealth situations. The sessions with the psychologist help clients who may be experiencing guilt, fear, anger, or shame for receiving money they feel they didn't "earn." Without exploring the reasons behind these feelings, sudden wealth recipients could find themselves having a hard time making decisions that are necessary in managing their new windfall.

Five years after the accident, Hank and Tracey have settled in to their new normal. Although they are millionaires, they continue to work as before. They regularly see their quarterback and the other advisors on their team to discuss ongoing plan performance and to listen to suggested strategies that might enhance their overall plan. They both met with a psychologist for a few sessions and now highly recommend the process to anyone whether a sudden wealth recipient or not.

They continue to deal with the challenges in front of them. They are happily involved with Zach's baseball team. Hank is the head coach, and Tracey is team mom. Tracey is pregnant and due in six months. It's a girl.

"Patience and perseverance have a magical effect before which difficulties disappear and obstacles vanish."

John Quincy Adams

ANALYSIS OF *HAPPINESS IN THE REARVIEW MIRROR*

by Pam Monday, Ph.D., LMFT, LPC

Life changing traumatic injury. Can you even imagine that happening to you?

One moment you have a wonderful life, active, healthy, happy—and in a flash of an instant, all that is torn from you. You wake up in the hospital, unable to move your body. Or perhaps you can't see, or hear, or feel anything. When you regain consciousness, you discover that life as you know it is over. All of your hopes and dreams are shattered. You feel absolutely overwhelmed with grief, rage, hopelessness.

There is no way to prepare for such trauma. But Hank had something that all of us need to heal—his family and friends who supported him. This family had some real strengths—commitment, deep love, the financial means to continue to pay the bills, even though it was hard when he was unable to work. Not everyone has this kind of support and help, and some simply never recover from depression and despair such tragedy brings.

Hank's story describes the stages that people go through when they are dealing with the overwhelming challenges of life as a handicapped person. He speaks of his embarrassment of being the center of attention, but this time not for his accomplishments. He has so many questions, but his friends don't really understand because they can't possibly fathom what he is going through. Everyone is trying their best; but all feel awkward and unsure. Hank clings to the belief at first that certainly he will walk again. But soon he begins to sink into depression as he faces the reality that he will be paralyzed forever. Next comes the despair as this strong man feels the shame of not being able to provide for his family, and his guilt and inadequacy as a man that his wife has to help him do everything and also carry the entire burden of responsibility for all the things he did for the family before. His loss of self sufficiency and independence show up as anger and frustration as he tries to mask his vulnerability.

After a while, he begins to accept his circumstances, and is able to begin to do what he can do and he begins to feel more hopeful. His reframe of "I am ABLE to work," is much more positive than saying "I don't HAVE to work." He is working hard to be a good husband and father, and rebuilding his self esteem as he finds ways to be more independent. His gratitude about being alive is a signal that he is really beginning to heal emotionally. Crucial to this healing is the ongoing support of his wife and family.

When I see someone in my office who has experienced this kind of trauma, I immediately assess the kinds of support networks they have. Did the couple have a strong marriage before the accident? If not, what is the state of the marriage now, with all of the incredible stresses? Did the spouse recognize how much they would have missed their spouse if he or she had died? If so, have they recommitted to loving and supporting, in sickness as well as in health? What other kind of support does the family have—extended family, good friends, a church community? Families need a lot of support to strengthen and comfort them, and this is needed for a long period of time. I call this period "mobile grief"—the person is not dead, but is not alive in the same way as before. It takes a long time for the individual, and the family, to work through all of the losses and challenges they face and begin to feel more hopeful.

People who have a history of being able to cope effectively in the face of life's normal transitions and challenges are at an advantage when this kind of traumatic injury occurs. They are more resilient emotionally because they have effective coping skills, such as being able to talk openly about what they are experiencing, and are able to grieve together. If the couple or family has difficulty talking about their internal experiences when ordinary challenges are faced, it becomes virtually impossible for them to support one another when trauma happens. Each person, in their grief and pain, withdraws from meaningful interactions and connections. They may isolate, or if not, still feel terribly alone even when in the presence of other family members. People may feel chronically angry as they attempt to bury or numb the pain, and some may begin to abuse alcohol or drugs in a desperate attempt to feel better. Children's feelings are often overlooked, as they see their parents suffering and they don't want to make things worse. But inside they feel alone and afraid if no one is talking to them about what they are experiencing. They may begin to have serious social, emotional or academic problems, or even get in trouble with the law.

If you have ever experienced any of these things in your family, I want you to know that help is available. A good therapist understands what you might not be able to express, and can teach you how to begin to open up and share so that you can feel the relief from pain that connection brings. You will be able to learn new things that will help you find support and resources in the community to lighten your burden. There are many wonderful organizations that can help you with moving through this type of life circumstance, and your therapist can help you find those resources.

Hank's story mentions the enormous medical costs associated with traumatic injury. Sometimes the complications from the injury continue throughout the individual's lifetime and are unpredictable. Most families who experience these kinds of losses are able to find a lawyer to help them file for damages. Money of course can't restore our old way of life, but it is the only means for us to feel some sort of justice for the terrible injustice that has happened to us. Unfortunately, it can take a long time for these cases to settle and funds to be distributed—even longer if you have to go to court. If, while you are waiting for money to arrive, you do not have sufficient financial resources for day-to-day living, the hopelessness, despair, and chronic financial stress can destroy your family. This is so serious that it is absolutely crucial that the family seek therapy as soon as possible to stop the descent into dysfunction that is inevitable with chronic stressors of any kind. Good therapy helps people find new ways to cope and new ways to strengthen a sense of hope and optimism within yourself and between you and your family members.

And finally, but of utmost importance, know that the people who are able to recover from the devastation of traumatic losses have faith that there is a loving and merciful God who can help them recover and give them a sense of hope. Do not be afraid to talk about your spirituality with a therapist! Sometimes the inevitable thought of "why did this happen to me?" results in extreme guilt as you agonize over what you might have done to deserve this tragedy. Or you might find yourself furious with God, or even convinced that surely He does not exist. Hold on to your faith, and talk about it with your pastor, your therapist or anyone else who can support you and help you find peace.

ROOTS

"When you take responsibility on your shoulders there is not much room left for chips."

Anonymous

Nathan and his business partners couldn't be any more different. Nathan Garza operated as the face of their company, and his two partners, James Roland and Todd Nugio, both software engineers, worked very much behind the scenes.

As the "deal" came closer to completion, James and Todd continued to keep themselves occupied with existing projects in the pipeline. The two of them were seldom influenced by the upcoming "life-changing event." They wanted nothing to do with the limelight that would follow this transaction. This transaction was big, they knew, maybe not on a global scale but big enough to make them very well known in the gaming industry in the United States. Both painfully quiet and private, they would accept this and move on. Their lives would not change.

Nathan, on the other hand, had very different ideas. As the CEO of the company, he was very much involved in the negotiations and was absorbed with the attention he was receiving lately in both the industry and the press. At thirty-six years old, he found the new life ahead of him occupied his mind lately as much as the actual transaction itself did. Eleven years out of graduate school and he was about to become a very wealthy man. A player, he thought, was how he would be described when his name came up among the leaders in the gaming software community. That MBA was finally paying off, he mused.

The event had been months in negotiations, and he knew that he had led his company to a level of success not reached by many young executives. He was going to be in many exclusive clubs moving forward.

Becoming a multimillionaire was a far cry from Nathan's family home in the outskirts of small-town USA. His family would not be considered poor, but wealth was not a word used to describe them in any way. His dad, the local postman, and his mom, a homemaker, had instilled in him and his five siblings an attitude of determination to excel unmatched by many others. As the youngest, Nathan benefited from this message being constantly ingrained in each of his brothers and sisters. At times he was intimidated by their fierce dedication to success and the high level at which they executed their dreams. His two brothers and three sisters held the following occupations: doctor, lawyer, lawyer, tenured professor, research scientist, and CEO of a software company (Nathan). Each had gone to a different but equally prestigious university for their fields. The family debate as to which was the best university in the country would forever monopolize their conversations at holidays and special occasions. Each of them had gained full academic scholarships, except for Nathan. Nathan's grades had secured him only partial scholarships at his chosen school, although he might have gotten a full ride at several other schools. He would have to work to pay for the rest of his costs. Two of his oldest siblings generously offered some financial backing if he needed it. He happily took them up on their offers on more than one occasion while he was in school.

Nathan, James, and Todd started Gaming Amigos seven years ago. For over a year, they had worked out of an incubator for start-up technology companies before developing two games that put them on the map. Finally having their own office space made them feel as though they had arrived, even though the revenue they were generating barely supported them. Still they were doing things their way and were determined to make a mark in the gaming world.

Five years after they started the firm, they created a highly popular series of games and earned them attention from larger companies. It was then that Nathan started taking a few calls related to a possible buyout from larger companies, but in his view, most of the interaction boiled down to "putting out feelers."

Nathan

I was flattered when the calls started coming in, but at the end of the day, no one seemed serious about actually buying us. They were feeling things out, trying to get an impression on our intent. Most, if not all, of them were just trying to see if we would even consider selling. Selling the company was something we hadn't talked about very much, but after a few more calls came in, I wondered if we did sell, how much we might bring. I began consulting with a couple of companies to inquire on a realistic value for our company. After a few months, we came to the conclusion that our little company could possibly sell for a large amount of money. I called the guys in for a meeting.

James

It's no secret the roles we play at Gaming Amigos. We kid Nathan all the time that Todd and I are the talent and he is our agent. We're joking, of course, because Nathan has crazy skills on the business side and has led the company very well all this time. Sometimes he has a tendency to be a bit overdramatic, so the morning he called us in for "another life-changing meeting," we kind of just rolled our eyes and thought, "Now what?"

Todd

James is spot on. The two of us are very content to create new games, and we spend most of our days in the studio doing what we love, creating games. We have always counted on Nathan to handle the business aspects of the company. We sometimes feel bad because while James and I work side by side and have each other to commiserate with on a bad day, Nathan has always been on his own island. He has always had a flair for the dramatic, but when he called us in that morning, he was very calm and had this strange smirk on his face, like he knew some big news and wanted us to get it out of him.

Nathan

I admit I have a tendency to let my enthusiasm dictate some of my decisions. However, this time, things felt differently. This time the news I was about to share with my partners was just "math." I had done the research, and I had the research confirmed twice. True, negotiations and the right buyer would be critical, but it was real news and the amount of money was a bit startling.

James

We just sat there sort of stunned when Nathan said $65 million to $75 million. We knew we were doing very well and certainly understood that larger companies in the industry might be interested in acquiring us, but $75 million sounded like Nathan's enthusiasm was getting ahead of him. But he sounded so sure that I became excited and nervous at the same time.

Todd

We've all known each other for a long time, so it's true that we make fun of Nathan's enthusiasm at times, but that morning he was so calm and confident. He showed us the numbers and the summaries by the two companies that did the analysis on the company evaluation. He showed us a list of companies he had spoken with in the past year. He most importantly showed us the short list of companies he had spoken to on more than one occasion. It sounded like a viable situation. We actually could sell our company for a lot of money. It sounded cool. I just said, "Okay, now what?"

Nathan

With all of us in agreement that we would explore the possibilities of selling, I returned calls to four of the companies that had expressed interest for a sit down. Two of the companies indeed were "just fishing" and eliminated themselves fairly quickly in the process. The other two were ready to make a deal. The next year was the craziest year of my life. I spent every waking hour with analysts from the other two firms. One of the firms utilized an office in our space and camped out for a good three months going over our financials and doing its due diligence. I rarely saw my wife. I spent all my time researching the possibility of selling the company. I needed to remain calm and strong in the negotiation. To be honest, in my mind, I had already sold the company and was ready to move on to the next stage of my life as a very wealthy person. I couldn't stop my mind from wondering about what I would do next, what my life would look like with all of that money. I used those thoughts to motivate me and keep me solely focused on making the sale happen. Negotiations quickly became serious but went back and forth for four months. Having two companies interested in acquiring you seems at first glance like a good thing, but going through the process with interested buyers just meant twice the number of meetings, twice the number of questions. By the time we finalized negotiations, I have to admit, I was spent. But it was worth it.

Fifteen months after deciding to explore the possibilities of selling the company, we each received $18 million! Now I don't care who you are or where you come from, $18 million is a lot of money. And being in a family of doctors and lawyers and professors, this youngest kid had finally beaten them all. With one wire into my bank account, I became the wealthiest person in my family. I couldn't wait until Thanksgiving to remind them that baby brother wasn't such a screw-up after all!

According to the buy-out agreement, I was required to stay with the acquiring firm for twelve months, while Todd and James were asked to stay on for two years. They were thrilled because basically they would be able to do the exact same things they were doing before the sale, albeit $18 million richer. Todd and James really were unfazed by the whole new-wealth thing. I think the biggest plan they had talked about was to go to upstate New York with their families for a week or so. But for me, twelve months of hanging on to help with the transition seemed like an enormous amount of time. I had things I wanted to do, and I was ready to start my new life. I was certain that I could help them transition much quicker than twelve months, and since I wasn't used to working for someone else, it was no surprise to anyone when the twelve months actually turned into a seven month stint as a mutual agreement between me and "Newco."

I spent most of my time assembling a financial team. I spent a few weeks interviewing firms to help me manage my new fortune. I ended up selecting three very well known national firms with impeccable reputations for handling wealth and one local boutique firm that came highly recommended. I gave each of them 25 percent of my money to manage since I believe competition makes people perform at a higher level. Hey, look at me; I've always competed with five siblings and look where it got me!

Authors' comments

After hiring multiple financial teams to manage his "empire," as he called it, Nathan spent the next year looking for his next project, his next toy, his next house. He had to find ways to stay busy, and his wife, Jill, said she was thankful that she wasn't home much during this period.

Jill

You would think that earning a windfall of $18 million would carry someone for quite a while.

The two years after the sale of the company were a struggle for Nathan. His whole life, his image, his daily existence were so wrapped around that company for so long that when he didn't have that in his life anymore, he became a little lost. I tell people how relieved I was to have a career, because my life really didn't change that much. Oh sure, more opportunities were available because of our new wealth, but as a lawyer, my daily existence was the same. I suspected early on that Nathan might have trouble with his new life. I didn't realize just how big a struggle it would be.

At times, he was like a caged animal. He needed to stay busy, so he looked at new houses, or possible changes to our current home. He bought a new Mercedes, which was very nice but very expensive. He shopped for boats, and eventually bought one that I thought was more appropriate for a single and much younger man than Nathan. We kind of discussed it, but by the time he showed it to me, he had already placed a down payment on it. At the time, I just gave in because he would be the one spending the most time on it, since he wasn't working, and I guess deep down I felt like he had earned the right to pick whichever boat he really wanted.

We also joined "the" country club in town, as Nathan decided to take up golf. I had no objection to this as it seemed like a good idea in spite of a hefty initiation fee. In reality, we could now afford things that in the past we would have never considered. However, when Nathan started looking into buying interest in a jet, I did put my foot down. It's not like we travel that much, and certainly when we do, we could still travel commercial. I told him we could travel first class if that would make him feel better, but I absolutely said no to buying a jet. Nathan started spending a lot of time away, as he would fly to Las Vegas for the weekend or spend the day on the boat but would end up coming home quite late. I might have suspected he was having an affair, but Nathan had a strong upbringing, and it wasn't in his nature to cheat. I trusted him but was concerned about how much time he was spending alone.

Then the economy started floundering, and he spent quite of bit more of his time in meetings with our financial firms. I didn't attend many of these meetings, as it's his expertise, but as the economy grew worse, his stress levels seem to rise quite a bit. I told him that we didn't have anything to worry about, but I wasn't able to convince him otherwise. It wasn't until several months later when he told me that we were down 36 percent that he caught my attention. I asked him how that was possible given the reputation of the firms we were working with, and he didn't really have a good answer. As it turns out, while each firm was investing aggressively, no one was overseeing our entire financial plan. Somehow, after taxes, losses, and spending, our $18 million payday had turned into a little over $8 million. Now $8 million is still more money than most people know what to do with, but for Nathan, it was like watching half his empire disappear before his eyes. He was angry and said we need to fire every firm and start over. There was no convincing him otherwise. We fired four firms in two days, and left over $8 million sitting in three bank accounts. Again, that is still a lot of money, and we should be thankful for what we have. For Nathan, he became very quiet and reserved. He started sleeping late, which was very unlike Nathan. I was worried that he was depressed. I called a few people for help.

Twenty-three Months after Selling the Company
Jill

I invited Todd, James, and Nathan's dad, Bill, to the house for a "pseudo" intervention. I wanted Nathan to know how proud of him we were and that we were concerned he was drifting from his roots. He hadn't spent much time with any of them recently. I thought just their presence alone would lift his spirits. As it turned out, it might have saved him.

Bill

My son has always carried a bit of a chip on his shoulder. As our youngest, he's had to walk behind his brothers and sisters who have done some pretty amazing things with their lives and careers. We always thought that Nathan would also do great things as long as he didn't sabotage himself. I don't know why, but he has a tendency to be very hard on himself.

That's why when Jill called, I came right away to have a heart-to-heart with my son. I told him that he should consider himself a huge success and nothing less. He created a business, and then he sold that business, bringing him and his partners over $50 million. The fact that the market turned and he has less money than he had does not make him less of a success. Sometime things just happen. At the end of the day, he's still a millionaire several times over. I reminded him of his roots and told him to always remember where he came from. I told him to stay grounded. I told him to quit worrying about what other people thought and to just be himself. I told him I was very proud of him. I told him I love him unconditionally.

Todd

It had been a while since we had seen Nathan, which is unusual since we had seen each other every day for so many years. I was surprised to see him looking so down and unsure of himself. He just seemed depressed and lost. The fact that he had also lost a lot of money in the market was tough on him as well. He's the financial brain of the three of us. He seriously went and hired four firms to handle his "empire," as he called it. James and I hired one local boutique firm that provides a lot of services, but we also told them we wanted to be conservative with our investments so we haven't lost much at all, and we don't worry about it. We've kept things pretty simple financially speaking. I never wanted the headache Nathan had from talking to a bunch of different financial firms. I didn't want to become a prisoner to my money.

James

I was shocked to see Nathan in such a state. He's always been our rock star, the guy who keeps us happy, and always upbeat. He's our boy, and I hated seeing him so down.

You know, some of the best advice we received after the buyout was when our financial advisors suggested we each meet with a therapist to discuss whatever feelings we had about our new wealth. Now knowing me and Todd and how much we hate talking, the idea of sitting down for a few sessions with a shrink to discuss our feelings was way down on the priority list. However, I took their advice and made myself do it. It actually was beneficial, so I told Todd he should do it as well. We each ended up going regularly for close to a year. The counselor helped me with many issues, some I didn't even know I had. In the end, she helped me be okay with the fact that I just want to be conservative in my life, with the money, and how I use it, how I invest it. I'm a pretty simple guy and she helped me learn to be okay with that. The whole thing was a freeing experience, and it was an experience that I shared with Nathan that day. I highly encouraged him to make an appointment with my therapist. I told Nathan that we were very appreciative of what he had done for our families, and I told him that we wanted to work with him again. I told him that we needed to work with him again, not necessarily to build and sell another company for a lot of money but because we work so well together and because, well, we're friends!

The rest of the story

Nathan received a wake-up call that day from his friends and family. They helped him see that perhaps there might be an easier way to live, and he clearly heard them say that perhaps he needed to be easier on himself. He heard them say to slow down and enjoy what he had created. He heard them remind him to be himself and remember where he came from.

He took their advice and made an appointment with the therapist. He's been going twice a month for the past six months and is now enthusiastic when he talks about his care and what he's learning about himself.

Financially, he and Jill decided to move to the same firm that his partners hired. Although he struggles sometimes with wanting to take more risk, for now, he is invested very conservatively, and he and Jill are just fine with that.

The three friends are working to start their next firm, which has them all very excited about the future.

Authors' comments

It's easy to assume that sudden wealth can take care of all of our problems. However, unresolved emotional issues can spring to the surface amid the excitement of the newfound wealth. These issues, left unresolved, can leave the suddenly wealthy bankrupt emotionally and financially. It is often a good practice to speak to an experienced psychologist early on to explore emotional issues that could possibly harm the decisions that need to be made for their newfound wealth.

It's also easy to assume that hiring multiple firms is better than hiring one. Many sudden wealth recipients feel their money is more diversified if they hire multiple firms. However, many times the multiple firms are actually managing their portion of the overall wealth in a very similar fashion to the others, while neither of them is privy to what the other firms are doing. Without someone to oversee the entire plan, the investor is susceptible to having a portfolio that is managed more aggressively than they may want. Multiple sources of aggressive investing could shock an investor in market cycles that are particularly volatile with long periods of negative returns.

Finally, the sudden wealth recipient needs to understand that the first rule of managing wealth should be to preserve the wealth. Understand that it is okay to go slow, to be conservative initially and, perhaps, always. It's okay to keep things simple. Do not become a prisoner to your wealth.

> "A man without principles never
> draws much interest."
>
> *Unknown*

ANALYSIS OF *ROOTS*

by Pam Monday, Ph.D., LMFT, LPC

I love working with entrepreneurs! They are the movers and shakers of the world, and have so many skills and talents. I see many men like Nathan in my therapy office, and it is exciting to help the Nathans of the world break free of some of the old rules they have learned that can drag them down when they want to be lifted up.

Nathan's large, successful family taught him rules that guided his behavior, such as work hard, be driven to excel, compete to be the best, your value as a person is based on career success and how much money you make. Our family is our "tribe," and we are loyal to our tribes, for sure. All families pass down rules that guide and direct our behaviors. And the rules Nathan learned helped him be a success, for his family demanded excellence. But even the best rules often have a downside. For Nathan, as for many entrepreneurs, the "rules" of being successful include being driven to be better than the others, to make more money than the others, to work all of the time, and to be constantly experiencing the adrenaline rush that running a company can produce. Caught up in this excitement, what suffers is often one's marriage, family life, and the experience of being present and enjoying all the other things life has to offer. And when the deals are done, and the money has been made, then what? Men come to my office feeling lost, depressed, and not knowing what to do with themselves when they sell their companies and no longer have their exciting work to define them. Their self esteem has been established by what they do, and when they are no longer "doing" the game, they often feel worthless and bewildered.

Men are often taught that it is weak to ask for help. That's why it is hard to get men to come to therapy! I ask men to tell me about sports they have played. How did they get better at it? Yes, they had to practice, but how did they learn? Many men tell me about their favorite coaches, the ones who helped them excel. I tell them that I am a coach, too, and that the things they can learn from me include understanding what rules they have been following all of their lives, and what rules are creating some problems for them that they might like to break from this point on. When we start talking about the rules and myths that they have learned—from their families, their cultures, their institutions—they begin to see things about themselves that they never realized before.

Now you may be wondering right now "what if what I realize about myself, I don't like?" That's where I come in with this: "You are a unique, special person. You have many gifts and talents, some of which you might not even know about. Would you like to discover those things? And then there are some things about you that others might be able to see and you can't; or that you are afraid that if others see it, they won't approve; or maybe if you feel you have to be perfect, you are afraid that you will look foolish or be ashamed if you discover something about yourself that you don't like. All of us have those fears! And guess what? All of us have new things to learn! We can't know what we don't know! But when we learn things we never learned before, we can grow and change and be happier in life than we've ever been before. How would you like to be happier?"

Nathan did not know that his self esteem suffered because he was always comparing himself to others, just like he had learned to do in his family. When we learn to be fiercely competitive, we are hard on ourselves. We beat ourselves up if we don't do it perfectly. We can't admit we make mistakes, we need to "look good" all of the time and life is a game of "you either win or you lose." That's exhausting! But even more troubling is that when we have a chance to relax and enjoy the fruits of our labors, we can't! Nathan didn't feel good about himself with nothing to do—and all he knew to do was work! He didn't have hobbies, he didn't do volunteer work—he was a captain without a ship. He knew how to get an adrenaline rush—spending that money on Vegas vacations and toys is an adrenaline rush! Thank goodness his wife put her foot down when he almost bought the plane! And remember, if our self esteem is based on how much money we have, then when we begin to lose money, we feel it is a reflection on us. Somehow, it's our fault, even when things happen over which we have no control (like the market dropping). Trying to regain control, we often become angry and try to find someone else to blame for our misery. Nathan lashed out and fired the financial firms, but that didn't help. He then became depressed. Depression is when we feel powerless, worthless, listless and even things that used to interest us, no longer do. This was Nathan's bottom, and fortunately his family and his friends came to his aid.

Family members often call me to have me help them help one of their loved ones. If their loved one does not want to come in with them to talk about their concerns, then I meet with as many of the family and friends as possible, and I give them strategies for what they might do to help. Nathan's family came together to do a loving "intervention". His wife invited his Dad and his partners to meet with him. They each shared their love for him, beginning with his dad. His Dad knew that Nathan had always competed with his siblings to "win" and be the best of them all. By doing this Nathan was too hard on himself and that trait would interfere with him achieving all that he wanted to achieve! How wonderful it was to have his father tell him that he was loved unconditionally—which means he was loved not for what he accomplished, but for who he was as a person! In the competitive environment of his family, this was a message that Nathan had not heard as a child. Dad told him it was okay to relax and enjoy his life, and to stop comparing himself to others. He could change! His partners told him about their experiences with their therapists, and how helpful it was. Nathan was able to hear their advice to go see a therapist, and learn about other things about himself that he could change.

I routinely invite people to bring in their family members—spouses, parents, siblings, whoever— so that we can learn together what rules have guided our behaviors throughout their lives, and what rules are passed down across the generations. Good therapy helps us be all that we can be, and I'll bet Nathan is happier than he has ever been, and can finally enjoy that sudden wealth!

DOCTOR, HEAL THYSELF

"Divorce is the one human tragedy that reduces everything to cash."

Rita Mae Brown

Karen and Bob were high school sweethearts and graduated from the same college. They were married three weeks after graduating from State U. Karen continued on to medical school and became a pediatrician. Bob continued his studies ultimately receiving an MBA (Master of Business Administration) and CPA (Certified Public Accountant) license. They had three kids, ages fifteen, twelve, and eight, in private schools. They lived in a fabulous home in the suburbs. Their lives were filled with their kids' soccer, baseball, and gymnastics. Heavily involved in the community, they could often be seen at non-profit galas, and each served on two boards for non-profit organizations. From the outside, they were the perfect citizens and the perfect couple living a perfect life.

Perception aside, twenty-two years later, they found themselves in mediation and likely headed to divorce court. Bob told Karen one weekend morning that he needed out, had hired an attorney, and was filing for divorce. With Bob's background, he had always handled the financial matters. As Karen's medical practice continued to grow, she rarely had the time or the desire to get involved with budgets, financial planning, taxes, life insurance, or things like "the market". She was content to be an excellent doctor and a leader in the community.

Karen

Growing up, Daddy always took care of the "money things." My mom stayed at home raising the five of us, and Daddy worked as a pharmacist and paid the bills. Paying the bills every month always seemed so stressful for him. He would be behind closed doors and get very quiet for hours. He was unavailable and seemed angry. I always felt like I had done something wrong or was a financial burden for my parents. I made straight A's in high school so I could get a scholarship to help them out with the money. I even took out school loans to attend medical school.

When Bob and I got married, he seemed to love paying the bills, handling budgets, and trying to find ways for us to save on taxes. He was always energized by anything financial, and I was so relieved and happy not to have to deal with any of that.

In my practice, I have a business manager who basically runs the show for me. I normally don't get involved with personnel or administrative issues. All I've ever wanted to do was to be a doctor, and being a pediatrician, I get to combine my love of medicine with my love for children. I make good money, but mainly I'm doing what I love. I've been able to leave the business matters to other people.

Now Bob wants a divorce, and I'm afraid I don't have a clue how much money I need to live on, let alone how much I should get in a divorce settlement. Other than my attorney, who also has no financial background, I'm not sure where to turn. I've asked friends if they know a good planner or broker, and I get different answers from different friends. What almost bothers me as much as the divorce is that no one seems to understand that although I'm an educated person, I am embarrassed to tell anyone how naive I am with financial matters. I read recently that 80 to 90 percent of women over their lifetime either by divorce or through the death of their husband will end up solely responsible for the financial decisions[3]. Reading statistics like that, how could I be so stupid?

I'm trying to be strong for my children and run my practice, but now also find myself trying to

---

3   U.S. Department of Labor estimate, 2010 <http://www.dol.gov/>.

maneuver through a world of finances that not only confuses me but also brings up many childhood issues that apparently I haven't dealt with before. All of those emotions of watching my dad pay the bills, and the guilt I felt comes flooding back. To top it off, I'm so angry with Bob for doing this to us! Twenty-two years of marriage and he decides that he needs a change. I don't remember that line being in our marriage vows! We have three beautiful children and a wonderful home. What could be so bad about our lives that he feels the strong desire to turn everything upside down? I know women recover from divorce every day, but if I don't find a good advisor, I'm afraid I'm really going to mess this up. I am riding a roller coaster of emotions; all severe, and I fear it's affecting my kids and my ability to make decisions, especially financial decisions!

Authors' comments

Karen is typical in that many people ask their neighbors, friends, or colleagues if they know any financial advisors. The challenge of being in Karen's shoes is that she and others like her often don't know the difference between an insurance agent, a wealth manager, an asset manager, a broker, or any of the other many different titles used in the financial world. They don't know whom to trust. They don't understand the significance of all the different letters or designations that follow many financial professionals' names. They don't know what questions to ask. They don't know who to interview to assist them, and they don't understand the myriad of products that are proliferating in the investment and insurance industry. The overall result of all of these unknowns is fear. They are fearful of making a mistake, fearful of admitting they need help. In the meantime, they are wrought with fear over the financial decisions, while struggling with emotional turmoil of the divorce and the breakup of their family.

In many divorce situations, the financial questions typically occur after the divorce is final. Why is that? Doesn't it make sense to enlist the support and guidance of an experienced, credentialed financial advisor before the divorce proceedings begin or at least before they get too far in the process?

The rest of the story for Karen

In spite of Karen's insecurities about financial issues, she was determined to seek financial guidance immediately. She created a plan of action. She wrote it down and still wondered if she could actually take control of her own financial life. She obtained the names of three experienced financial professionals in her area. She then asked other professionals, friends, and particularly other women, who had also been through divorces recently, if they knew any of the three firms. Her plan was the following:

- Create a budget (what will it cost to live on my own with the kids?)
- Call George, Jeaneane, and Sandy for recommendations of financial advisors
- Set up meetings with each advisor within the next three weeks
- Ask Cindy if she knows a good estate planning attorney

- Schedule meeting with estate planning attorney by the end of the month
- Open bank account
- Interview CPA firms
- Buy and read two or three books on investments
- Create list of questions to interview advisors

Karen

Three firms were recommended to me by various people. Of the three firms, one was a large national firm my business manager worked with in the past; one, an insurance agent and friend of a friend; and another, a private firm with experience in divorce cases referred to me by my best friend Sandy. Each came highly recommended, so I feel pretty good that I'll end up with someone who knows what they are doing. I guess I'll know more after I interview them. I wrote down my mini list today and it isn't looking so "mini!" I have so much to do, I may have to take some time off to get it all done, but my patient schedule is booked solid for the next month!

Authors' comments

Karen starts out with the right idea by writing down a list of to-do's. However, oftentimes these lists can get rather long and seem impossible to complete. As you can see in her case, she wondered how she would ever find the time. This is also common as the investor doesn't realize that although they have created a list, they may not know which item should come first. They may not realize that certain firms that focus on sudden wealth issues, like divorce, have created processes to consolidate some of these items, which can save the client countless hours of planning and interviewing.

Karen

This is taking so much longer than I thought it would! I interviewed the life insurance guy who seems nice enough but has only been in the business for seven years, so I wonder if he has enough experience for my situation. He also works out of his house so that felt a little awkward to me. His prime focus was life insurance, but he didn't seem vaguely knowledgeable or interested about anything else.

Last week I met with a private independent firm. I really liked the fact that the principals of the firm had been in the business for a long time and had great experience and credentials. They seemed to really listen to me, and they even had a process for helping individuals going through all types of "sudden wealth" (their term) situations. I laughed and commented that because of the cost of a divorce, it should be called "suddenly less wealth," but they reassured me that the fact that this is more money than I have ever been responsible for personally, it was "my sudden wealth." I thought and prayed about it and hired them the next day. I didn't even keep the interview with the third firm, because this just felt right.

Nine Months Later
Authors' comments

Karen hired the independent firm who went right to work. They created a plan of action and reassured her that they would help her with priority and pace for each item to be completed. They helped her interview CPAs and attorneys. They created a financial plan based on her budget so she could include this in her negotiations with her attorney and her husband's attorney. They recommended a banker to help her get a new credit card and bank account. They suggested she avoid making any major purchases for one year. They collaborated with her attorney on all financial issues related to her divorce. Divorce negotiations went smoothly and were settled after only five weeks. She feels good about the settlement of almost $2 million, as it is less than $30,000 from the number in her financial plan. The fact that she had a financial plan put her at ease when negotiations began. The idea that she wasn't asking for everything from her husband put him at ease. Because of this, the typical hostilities of divorce proceedings were minimal. Her money was managed in a fairly conservative strategy, as requested by her, consistent with the findings of the original financial plan. She meets with her team every four months and has access to them via phone and e-mail whenever she needs them. She often will ask them for education on the investment strategies they are executing. Karen considers her advisors key confidants in every financial decision she makes.

She is financially prepared and is confident in her team and confident in understanding the strategies that are being executed and the reasons behind it. Although she still struggles with anger toward her husband, she challenges herself to remain cordial for the sake of the children. She is considering writing a book for doctors who find themselves divorced and financially "ignorant." She remains devoted to her children and the circus of their many activities. She has started dating again.

Bob remarried (another doctor!) who brought two young children to his blended family.

> "He that can't endure the bad will not live to see the good."
>
> ***Yiddish Proverb***

ANALYSIS OF *DR. HEAL THYSELF*

by Dianne Arnett, M.A., LMFT, LPC

We all start our marriages with hearts filled with hopes of opportunity! Wedding days are full of joy, new beginnings and dreams of future adventures and growing old together! But when those dreams unravel so do our lives. Facing divorce at any time is devastating and one of the most challenging times anyone faces. Lives are thrown out of balance as relationships with friends and family are fractured, financial security is threatened and a seemingly endless number of changes occur simultaneously. There is not a way to paint a pretty picture or soft pedal this challenge! Divorce has a ripple effect and touches the lives of everyone who knows the family. Support at this time is crucial! Friends, family, ministers and counselors will all be of comfort to any individual, couple and family experiencing this enormous transition. People not only survive divorce, but they are able to thrive in their new lives afterward!

We don't know how much effort Bob and Karen put into saving their marriage. It seems to have been Bob's unilateral decision. Divorce is a monumental decision. I work with men and women individually as well as couples who are facing the decision of separation. I encourage couples to do everything possible to mend their broken relationships so that even if they must divorce they can live with few regrets. This approach eases the pain if they ultimately get to the point of a permanent separation. We collaborate on ways to behave with respect, maintain dignity and build a future of little regrets. This decision is best made as a couple since collaboration makes for a smoother divorce and life afterward, especially if children are involved.

Karen was caught completely off guard as she was leading what she considered a very productive, fulfilling life. The unexpected divorce is even more difficult to face. Rejection is the greatest fear anyone faces in any relationship. Friends and family are shocked, too, when they hear the announcement that a couple is divorcing. This is especially true when it is a couple that they admired and thought had a solid relationship. This ripple effect often makes family and friends feel insecure about their own relationships or feel compelled to take sides. Divorce alone is overwhelming enough for anyone to accept and manage and is compounded further with the loss of some extended family and friends.

One of the most difficult elements after the decision to divorce is made is how to tell the children. This is a delicate conversation and requires a delicate approach. The day parents sit their children down and make this announcement is forever imbedded in a child's memory. We all have heard our adult friends reminisce about such conversations. They carry a lot of weight with a person for a long time. Children's sensitivities vary greatly. I strategize with parents on the gentlest approach for their children. Even the most loving, thoughtful parents find relief after a therapy session that results in an agreed upon approach for this life-changing conversation with their children. Parents must be prepared to answer all the questions that their children will immediately have in a reassuring manner. We strategize about these as well.

Children's lives are turned upside down overnight when they hear the news their parents are divorcing! It is an awful experience for them even under the most loving circumstances. Though rare, some children are relieved at this announcement if they have grown up in families with long-term, constant chaos and conflict. Relief may come immediately for these children, but does not eliminate the challenges that follow. Divorce has a lasting impact on children. Easing the trauma is important to parents. Having an objective, experienced professional helps avoid some unnecessary pain. The entire family benefits long term when the initial decisions are made thoughtfully and collaboratively. Managing each step of the divorce in a positive, healthy manner in regards to the children is crucial. The impact is felt immediately and definitely has an impact as the children enter adolescence.

Virtually all children take some responsibility for the breakup. Universally children believe that they had an impact on the marriage and influenced their parent's decision to split up. I have encountered some who feel that they were too much trouble, a strain on the busy lives of the family and even a financial drain on their parents. A little boy that I worked with just knew he had caused the divorce. He said, "If I had picked up my toys when my mommy asked me to she wouldn't be so unhappy." This comment was shocking to his parents yet enlightening to them about the importance of their reassurance. Children need an objective listening ear to help them process their feelings. Sometimes it is easier to share their honest feelings when their parents are not in the room. Children have a difficult time understanding their mixed emotions. They know they are not happy and know they do not like what has happened to their family, but often cannot get beyond that. They need help to figure it all out and it takes time. Children of all ages of divorce usually benefit tremendously from having a counselor help them through the many changes. I work with the family in different combinations.... sometimes a child alone, sometimes a group of siblings, sometimes one parent with the children and sometimes with the entire family. Different needs of each child and family requires different approaches. A good therapist will help the family identify and meet these needs.

One of the most significant contributions a therapist can have on a family going through divorce is to help with co-parenting. Parenting takes on a different format with two households. When done with the children's happiness and development as a priority it is easier for them to adjust to the changes and continue to have a happy, flourishing childhood! Greater financial resources and stability will ease some of the hardships of single-parenting. After a session or two with the parents independently to solidify their co-parenting expectations we come together and create plans involving living arrangements, discipline, and schedules and resolve any major decision making conflicts. It can be a win-win for everyone involved! Sometimes the parents can manage the execution of the plan on their own and sometimes they like to do it with me. This is a good time to bring the children into therapy. The children usually start out fairly quiet in family sessions, but as the sessions continue they become fully engaged. They not only like the safe setting to talk things through, they dominate the conversations! Therapy is a good stop in a life of major change!

While Karen perhaps had been in denial during her marriage about her disintegrating relationship, she took a reverse stance in her approach to her divorce. She was forced into action after Bob filed for divorce. She spoke with friends and family and sought legal and financial advisors. She became courageous in looking at topics that were intimidating to her in the past. She took the bull by the horns when it came to managing the unfamiliar financial elements as she hired financial advisors, a CPA and lawyer to guide her. I wonder if she sought out support from a professional counselor. People I work with are always surprised how hard divorce is on themselves, spouses, children, their own siblings, parents, in-laws and friends. They are also surprised how long it takes to finalize the legal portion and begin to move on emotionally. Letting go of the dreams of living happily ever after and accepting a new life takes time and requires patience for everyone who has been touched. Seeing the entire process through with a team of professionals makes the difficult process easier. The team approach offers the individual, couple in their new roles and the family as a whole time to heal in all areas.

After the dust settles, legal aspects are finalized and everyone has adjusted, life does move on. Lives are rebuilt, new friendships and relationships are made and people find strengths in themselves that they did not know existed. Sibling relationships are often strengthened, ex-spouses co-parent constructively together and the family team, while in a new form, is still a team. New houses, schools, careers, marriages and blended families may be on the horizon for Karen, Bob and their children. Growth, development and happiness after divorce are possible!

THE SOUNDS OF SILENCE

"Forgiveness is the final form of love."

Reinhold Niebuhr

Bobby stared blankly at his clasped hands, finding it difficult to fathom what had transpired over the last few weeks let alone five minutes ago. Sitting on a bench in the park right outside his grandfather's home he thought how he would give up everything to turn back the hands of time. Recently, the countless trips to the hospital had his mind racing with the memories that he and his grandfather had created over the 27 years of Bobby's life.

His grandfather, or "Bud", as he was taught to call him ever since he could talk, was one of his best friends. Since Bobby's father died when Bobby was four years old, they had become two peas in a pod. Why Bud and not grandpa? Bud always told everyone he could never be called "grandpa" because he would never be old enough to be called grandpa. So over the years the grandkids learned after several tries of "PAPA BUD", "G-PA BUD" that it was just "Bud".

Bobby and Bud both shared a love of the outdoors, particularly fishing on the river not far from the cottage that Bud had owned for 40 years. At least once a month the two "peas in a pod" would spend a couple of days fishing on the river bank underneath a huge willow tree. The fishing was usually productive as Bud had an uncanny ability to entice the fish to his line. Bobby had learned well over the years and once he became a teenager, the competition was on. As a child, the bets on who could catch the most fish started at 25 cents a fish, but as Bobby grew older, the ante became as high as $5 dollars a fish.

The bragging rights were always more important than the money. Without an official tally over the years, Bud would just explain to family and friends that he and Bobby's competition was "about even", he would say with a wink.

When Bud wasn't fishing with Bobby, he was a family doctor, who was revered by his patients. He always remembered that house calls weren't against the law, and if he had a patient in need after hours, he was usually there to help them. Married for 47 years to his wife Sarah before she died three years earlier, he had two daughters Samantha (Sammie) and Sandy, and three grandchildren Bobby 27, Karen 15, and Carla 12.

Bobby

Bud was like superman to our family. Even when he got sick, I never thought he was going to die. He was the greatest guy and a second father to me. I can't imagine my life without him. But for him to completely change his will to have just us grandkids as heirs is strange. I'm not sure how to handle all of this. My mom and aunt are so mad. They are acting like I had something to do with this and I had no idea he was going to do this. I certainly have no clue why he would skip my mom and my aunt in his will. With my cousin's inheritance going to their trusts, my aunt will at least have some say so over how the money is spent in their case, but in mine, it's a little crazy that I have three million dollars in my bank account and there's nothing my mom can do about it. I don't know, maybe he thought since I'm a banker that it would be better off in my hands over my mom's.

Samantha (Bobby's mother)

Daddy never said a word about his will over the last few months. Since Bobby's father died, he and my dad have been like father and son, and I was and am so appreciative of their special relationship but to ignore me and my sister in his final wishes is definitely confusing and hurtful. We've been so close especially after mom died and during the last few months when he was sick. Both my sister and I shared the load of his care without fail. We were there. We've always been there for mom and dad. The whole thing just feels like a bad dream.

Over the next few months after Bud's death, Bobby and his grieving family tried to move on with life. Bobby tried to cheer his mother up by buying her a new house. Total money spent on his mother's new home was over $400,000. As a banker, Bobby knew that mortgage rates were very low, but instead he paid cash for the house. The new house needed new furniture that Bobby also paid for – another $25,000. You would think that these acts of kindness towards his mother would end her deep anger and frustration toward her dad, but it did not. She and her sister would often meet for a cup of coffee or a margarita and continue the diatribe about their father and how he must have been out of his mind to do this to them. The fact that he took care of their children was noted, but it never squelched their thirst of wanting to know why he would forget his daughters. What message was he trying to send them? They felt dismissed.

Bobby didn't limit his spending on his mother. On the contrary, Bobby bought a downtown condo in an exclusive building. He was the proud resident of what he saw as the "perfect bachelor pad". For the rights to live in the perfect bachelor pad, Bobby paid $759,000 dollars. Impatient of the time it would take to close a mortgage and the fact that he thought it would be cool to write a check that large, he paid cash for his new home. In a very short period of time, his 3 million dollar bank account was reduced to 1.5 million dollars. Bobby didn't care. He figured with his salary at the bank of $150,000 and the money left over he was still set. There were more toys to buy. He was starting to enjoy his new lifestyle.

Bobby

It's amazing what being rich can do for the dating life. Everywhere I go now, there's a woman hitting on me. Sure, I bought a Porsche and live in a pretty plush condo, but I'm basically the same guy. I'm definitely not complaining. Life is good. Well, for the most part life is good. It seems I must be on every non-profit agency leads list, so I get a lot of calls from people asking for money. And even though I bought and furnished a new home for my mom, she still seems so angry at everything. It's not my fault that Bud excluded Mom from his will. It just seems like she's mad at him and he's not here so she takes it out on me. I try to be understanding, but I have to admit that I don't take half of her calls anymore. All she's going to do is complain anyway.

I've met some really cool people in my new building. I guess rich people just have more fun in general because a couple of my new buddies are serious partiers. We've been to Vegas twice in the last month and the parties were ridiculous! It's just like some of the movies or TV shows about the lives of the rich and the famous. Granted I'm not that rich and certainly not famous, but when I'm in Vegas it sure feels like it!

Rich (Bobby's best friend)

I've known my boy Bobby since high school. He certainly hasn't had an easy life with his dad dying when he was so young and being raised by his mom. His grandfather was kind of like a compass for him. What a great guy he was. Without his grandfather around, Bobby seems a little lost. Add on the fact that he has a lot more money now and all that wealth can bring, has me a little bit worried about Bobby. I went with him to Vegas last week and the amount of money spent was crazy. He paid for my entire trip and with our suite, drinks, and gambling, it was several thousand dollars. This guy that he knows from his building was also there and I'm not real sure about that guy. He comes from a very wealthy family which is fine, but I wouldn't label him as a "good guy". He's pretty slick and is into cocaine "recreationally" as he says. It also seems like some of the girls that were hanging around were into cocaine a little more than just recreationally. We've played around casually with drugs over the years, mainly marijuana and a little cocaine, so I don't think Bobby would ever get hooked on drugs, but he did seem to do more cocaine in that weekend than in his entire life, so hopefully that doesn't become a problem.

He was also dating this girl (Dana) for a few months before his grandfather died and he seems to have just blown her off completely. I liked her and I thought she was good for Bobby, but apparently he just lost interest. I asked him about it last week and he just said something stupid like they had grown apart. My girlfriend Stephanie has her radar up even higher and she is very worried about Bobby. She said he is acting and even looks reckless these days. She said he's not handling his grief in a healthy way. I don't know about all that, but I do know that he just doesn't seem his old self which is understandable given the circumstances. I even tried to get him to go fishing one weekend and he wasn't interested. Now that's pretty rare, Bobby not wanting to go fishing. He also bought that house for his mom and she's been kind of a bitch to him. I know that's wearing on him. All in all, he's dealing with a lot. I'm going to keep a close eye on him. I'm sure he'll be fine.

Dana (Bobby's ex-girlfriend)

I was dating Bobby for about four months before Bud passed away so I had a chance to meet Bud and understand he and Bobby's relationship. Even as Bud was sick, Bobby always sought approval and guidance from Bud. Bud treated me like family and that always made me feel really good about my future with Bobby. All of that changed however when Bud passed away.

I was there to console Bobby when Bud died. Bobby was crushed as you could imagine. Yet almost immediately after learning about the will, Bobby became standoffish towards me. As I tried to spend more time with him to help him cope with his loss and the new financial situation, he just ignored me. He ignored my suggestion to see a financial advisor, saying he was smart enough to handle it himself. I finally just left him alone for a few days just to give him some space. Later that week, I found out through a mutual friend that he was seen at a club flirting with more than one woman. Although I admit I was angry, I assumed that was his inconsiderate way of coping with his feelings. I called him to sort out everything and to see if the relationship could be worked out. I knew he was hurting.

Five Months after Bud's Death
Bobby

You would think that when an employee deposits 3 million dollars in the bank he works at, that employee would get something. A little respect, maybe a bonus, would be nice. That's definitely not the case here. My boss only wants to talk about my call list, what time I get to work and what time I leave. I feel like a slave. With everything I've been through in the last few months, I might just need to take a long vacation. Some of the guys have been talking about going to Vegas for a week. I might just join them and then stay another week by myself, that way I could just be off the grid for a while. I'm tired of everyone wanting a piece of me. I'm doing my best and that just doesn't seem enough.

Dana

Talking to him was ineffective. He just yelled at me when I mentioned seeing a therapist. He said he wasn't crazy and that I must be crazy to suggest he see a shrink! He told me he didn't need "people like me" in his life. He said I needed to let him live his life and never speak to him again.

Rich

I met Bobby for drinks this weekend. He seems like a totally different person. He's mad at the world. He spent a lot of time talking about his mom, and the bank and how they have done him wrong. He keeps rambling about deserving respect and he's not getting any. I'm also certain that he's doing a lot more cocaine these days. He's jittery and keeps tugging at his nose non-stop. I'm not really sure what I can do except listen, but it's getting to the point where I feel I need to do something or he could end up in a lot of trouble.

Eight Months after Bud's death
Samantha

I got a call from Bobby tonight. FROM JAIL! Apparently he was involved in some kind of road rage, racing incident. A police car happened to see it all and arrested him. As if that isn't bad enough, he had been drinking and they found cocaine in his car! I've had to hire a lawyer. Bobby's in a lot of trouble and he doesn't seem to care. He's always been a good kid, and lately I don't even recognize him. My dad was always such a calming influence on Bobby. Without him here, Bobby's just faltering at every turn. He's just not coping well with anything and I don't know what to do about it.

Bobby

I don't know why everyone is so bent out of shape. It's not like I killed anyone you know? Does anyone realize that my grandfather, my best friend, died less than a year ago? Yeah I realize that I was in jail and I have to go to court to get the charges dismissed, which I'm sure will happen since this is my first offense. Everyone is making a big deal out of every move I make these days. Mom is still mad at Bud for passing her up in the will and continues to take it out on me. My boss is jealous that I have more money than he does and he just tries to find ways to get me into trouble. All Rich does is give me lectures these days. The only peace I get is in Vegas which is where I'm heading. With millions of people in Vegas and that's the only place in the world where nobody bothers me. I don't need this shit. I'm gone.

Ten Days Later
Samantha

I found out through Bobby's best friend Rich that he was fired last week. I've called his cell phone; I've been to his condo. I've called hospitals and everyone I know who knows him. No sign of Bobby. I'm going out of my mind with worry. I called Rich again and he is getting on a plane right now to Vegas.

Rich

I'm not sure what I'm going to say when I find him. Nothing is getting through to him these days. I've spoken to some of our friends about an intervention and everyone seems on board with the idea. I just hope I'm not too late.

Final Comments

Bobby was found dead in his Las Vegas room of an apparent drug overdose. He was found by his best friend Rich and hotel security. Next to his body they found a bag of cocaine and an almost empty bottle of vodka. On his night stand was a check written to his mother for $834,000. In the memo section it read, "final payment". The check was not signed.

Authors Comments

You'll notice that unlike the other 7 stories, there are no author's comments mixed into the story of Bobby and his inheritance. Although a sudden wealth situation normally needs the guidance of a financial advisor who understands both the financial and emotional aspects of sudden wealth, sometimes the emotional toll is so extreme that a mental health professional is crucial to help the family member process their pain and learn to cope in a functional, productive way. For some, the pain of how they acquired their wealth can be so complex and so emotionally devastating that the idea of coping with financial challenges at the same time is overwhelming, and too much to bear. In this case, the unspoken, unclear communication will always haunt this family unless they get family therapy to resolve their grief. When these types of situations are recognized, we call our partners in psychology for guidance.

> "There is no grief like the grief
> that does not speak."
>
> *Henry Wordsworth*

ANALYSIS OF *THE SOUNDS OF SILENCE*

by Dianne Arnett, M.A., LMFT, LPC

The silence will weigh heavy in their hearts for the rest of their lives. In many of life's circumstances it is true that timing is everything. There could have been, should have been, would have been a different ending to Bobby's story. *If only…*

When I first learned of this tragedy I felt the overwhelming devastation each of these friends and family members have all been left to manage. It was as if an emotional tornado hit the family. The skies began to darken with Bobby's father's death years before, the storm hit with Bud's passing and will probation and then all was silent with Bobby's suicide. After Bud's death they were all so painfully swept up in their own emotions it was impossible for them to see clearly how others were also deeply impacted leaving them unable to empathize or respond in a supportive, constructive manner. They were each truly emotionally wounded for a multitude of reasons. If ever there were a family in need it was Bobby's family. The timing of such help would have been most powerful all the way back to the beginning of the first traumatic event: the death of Bobby's father. Support from others is the shelter through emotionally traumatic events in life.

If we could turn back the hands of time as Bobby wished for his grandfather on the day of Bud's death, and his family had sought professional guidance, both in the emotional and financial realms, they would have made many decisions differently. Seeking therapy can help soften the pain of daily issues and derail some terrible tragedies. While this story touches our hearts and the most glaring needs were emotionally driven we cannot underestimate the influence that a financial advisor might have made as well. With a controlled spending and investing pattern Bobby may have avoided many of the temptations and pitfalls that led to his mounting frustrations, poor decisions and ultimate death. This is a story of strong emotions impacted by bewildering financial decisions with unnecessary emotional decay and devastating loss.

Bud was born in the era when a man was taught to "pull himself up by his bootstraps". Taking Bobby under his wing and assuming the role of surrogate father was doing just that for Bud and Bobby. Therapy for older generations is usually equated with severe mental illness. Most individual's emotional behaviors and needs were discounted and discredited. The idea of a physically healthy man going to therapy was unheard of for the most part during Bud's generation. Certainly, such need or action would have been hidden in the deepest vaults of family secrets. I wonder how Bud emotionally dealt with the unexpected loss of his son-in-law and later his wife of so many years. Perhaps Bobby's mother, Sammie, was influenced by her father in this regard and too felt as if the family had it all under control at the time of her young husband's death....and some families do. Family generational patterns, beliefs and even myths carry a great deal of power in making decisions that impact the heart, mind and bank account. Each generation has the power to decide what rituals, traditions and values to carry forward, which to leave behind and which new ones to embrace.

Fortunately, the global impression of therapy is changing. Openness toward counseling has begun and continues to expand with each human story shared, as the ones in this book. The science of psychology and the profession of psychotherapy have been substantiated and given more credibility by brain studies for the past two decades. MRI [Magnetic Resonance Imaging] studies and clinical research have made therapy more acceptable and consequently, a source of support. Going to therapy is no longer an embarrassment. Some individuals, couples and families are even so bold as to openly share with family and friends their positive growth and development in therapy. Therapy is no longer about pathology or illness, but about learning to identify emotions, understanding yourself and others, and realizing how family history impacts present behavior. It is a process that enhances our opportunity to live the best life we are capable of living. Simply stated, in therapy we learn why people do the things they do and learn ways to do them better. More effective communication techniques are also learned. It is often not what one says, but how one says it that influences the outcome in any circumstance, conflict or relationship. In a counselor's office emphasis is given to the presentation of thoughts, feelings, hopes and desires. When conveyed in a more thoughtful manner a message, even an undesirable one, is more readily received. What impact might have been made upon Sammie, Sandy, Bobby and his cousins and even his friends had their thoughts, feelings and behaviors been examined in a different light?

The reason for Bud's decision to skip over his daughters is unknown and haunting. Bud had no sons and Bobby was his only grandson. I wonder if his family belief was that men manage money, after all Bobby was a banker. It could have been that simple. I wonder what a difference it would have made to each family member if Bud had left a letter explaining his decision. A financial advisor might have made such a recommendation or facilitated a family discussion changing the course of this family's future.

Reframing behavior and seeking alternative explanations is frequently done with a therapist when such a scenario is presented. A person can often be so wrapped up in his own rejection, like Sammie and Sandy, that he cannot conceptualize any fresh explanations for a particular behavior or incident. Making assumptions gets us all into trouble, and we all do it from time to time. We jump to conclusions without knowing the other person's motivations or intentions. We oftentimes believe the worst through our misinterpretations, catapulting future action in the wrong direction. Sammie and Sandy find themselves locked permanently in a place of rejection because they will never know for certain the reasons behind his decision. Such self-induced emotional life sentences do not have to become permanent, scarring our futures or causing subsequent damage. Misreading others may result in distancing, fracturing or losing relationships with those whom we love the most.

In my office we would talk about Bud's past decisions. We would look at Bud's family history, values, beliefs and behavioral patterns that might have influenced him to leave the money directly to Bobby. Perhaps Bud relied on Bobby to financially care for his mother as Bud had lovingly provided for the women in his family. We would also look closely at other ways that Bud and his wife showed their love and support to their two daughters throughout their lifetime. Identifying a lifetime of loving actions would enable Sammie and Sandy to free themselves from the negative evaluation of their father's love from his final, financial decision. Bud's love for his daughters is not defined by a single act, but a lifetime of interactions. Had this occurred I wonder, like you the reader, whether Sammie's resentment toward Bud would have persisted? The money Bobby received from Bud was not the catalyst for Sammie's suffering; it was the rejection she was left to manage with no absolute clarity or closure.

The timing of Bud's last will and testament may also have been an influential factor in his capacity to make a wise decision. It is possible that Bud's final decision may have been impacted by his physical health if done in his later years. Shane and David advise families that it is never too early to make decisions regarding estate planning. There are many possible reasons for Bud's decision and talking this out individually or in a family session with the two sisters or the entire family would likely have uncovered some of the mystery with the aid of a therapist's objective eye. Delving deeper into the family history helps to shed light on fresh perspectives. Healthier and new emotional states can be developed through such examination. Finding peace in the reasoning behind the inheritance decision may have lead to healthier interpretations and choices from them all. Interpretations, reactions and behaviors have a domino effect on one another. It is a challenge to avoid pushing over the first emotional domino when an individual, couple or family are overwhelmed by a comment, decision and especially an event as powerful as the one that impacted Bobby and his entire inner circle of family and friends.

The distribution of Bud's inheritance ultimately is irrelevant to the family after Bobby's suicide. Could Bobby's death have been prevented? Absolutely! A different outcome could have transpired with a different approach by all from the onset if Bobby was open to accepting support and care. Knowing when to intervene and how to engage an unwilling partner is one of the most difficult decisions for a family member who has recognized a need for professional help. Bobby's family and friends saw his suffering and witnessed his decline, but could not seem to stop the oncoming train wreck. They wanted to help, reached out until banned from his life and then left frozen as to what action or non-action would be most beneficial. It is common to withdraw when a person shuts you out of his life. There are people who reject support no matter what action is taken by family, friends and professionals. Analogous to a physician who cannot save a critically ill patient, it is also true that sometimes a person gets into such a severe psychological state that it is hard, even impossible, for a professional to pull a client through. As the dedicated physician will try every possible technique to save a patient to the last heartbeat, so, too will a dedicated therapist continue to attempt to save an emotionally suffering client. Timing has a great impact. As with physical maladies, emotional challenges are most successfully treated with early intervention. This is particularly true in the recovery from substance abuse. Depression, anxiety, and a wide-variety of other impairing emotional challenges are also more easily and successfully addressed with early intervention.

If you suffer or have a family member suffering from emotional challenges and you do not know what to do, how to handle it or how to engage your friend or family member into a therapeutic environment you are not alone. A therapist can assist you by giving you knowledgeable information to understand the issues and offer suggestions for a positive approach. Collaboratively with my clients I pursue treatment options based on individual and family openness, needs and resources. Most families can work through issues with in-office sessions, while addictions may require more extensive in-patient treatment.

Engagement challenges are not uncommon. It is often the family member who suffers the most who is most resistant to seek help. In daily challenges, as well as in the direst cases, when a family member refuses professional support a therapist can offer guidance on how to best support from within the family. Family support, like timing, has a critical impact on success. When a friend or family member is in greatest duress is when family support is most needed. Words of support, love and hope carry great power. As was true with Bobby, you, too, may be discounted, criticized or even rejected as you attempt to engage. It takes varying degrees of persistence and courage to repeatedly pursue unwanted intervention. Guessing wrong when you witness atypical behaviors of those you know may have irreversible results. Professionals can help evaluate the severity. Bobby's self-destructive behavior started mildly and escalated to more severe behaviors indicating his decline and desperation. The signs eventually became more obvious, but the family's debilitated state impacted their delay in action and profoundly cost them all. With professional intervention, Bobby might still be a contributing member to society, a banker, a friend, a son and perhaps even a husband and father. In this tragedy the family lost more than one family member; they lost the potential for a happier future. You can make a difference! Like Bobby's friends and family have learned through their tragedy...it is better to make a serious and persistent attempt to intervene repeatedly than live with the regret that you remained silent and wondering whether you could have been the one who touched a heart and changed a life-altering decision. Love and friendship, support and guidance are that powerful and influential. Renewed hope can be life changing. Bobby's friends and family were left with unresolved issues surrounding Bud's death and now face compounded grief with the loss of Bobby through suicide. I hope Bobby's friends and family have freed themselves from their own sounds of silence and made the call for support. When in doubt, take shelter from the storm, make the call......TODAY!

PART TWO

APPLICATIONS

BUILDING YOUR TEAM

"Coming together is a beginning. Keeping together is progress. Working together is success."

Henry Ford

Sudden wealth recipients face a unique set of challenges as they start to build their financial team. Unlike established, wealthy investors who may have had years to develop their investing philosophy or even have a structured family office to yield fiscal guidance and support, sudden wealth recipients are oftentimes starting from a clean slate. Sudden wealth recipients begin their journey with no established advisory relationships, and no defined investment philosophy or legacy plans. Add to the mix, needy family and friends (including some they haven't seen or heard from in years!), investment promoters on every corner, dozens of financial news networks and publications, and the roller coaster of emotions brought on by a sudden windfall, and the sudden wealth recipients are in a very precarious situation.

These stories have given you an inside look at many of the challenges sudden wealth recipients are facing. The Snows from chapter 3 thought they had a good financial relationship with their advisor but learned not all advisors are created equal. It may have taken some time, but the Hamiltons in chapter 5 and Hank and Tracey in chapter 9 found the right professionals to manage their sudden wealth. In chapter 13, Karen's fear grew from her sheer confusion about the financial services industry. Perhaps the path of Natalie in chapter 7 is most illuminating as her team expanded beyond financial services and into emotional counseling.

The fear and confusion of not knowing where to turn when faced with a sudden windfall are common denominators in each of these stories and for so many other people dealing with sudden wealth. Why is that? The financial services industry has been in existence for a very long time. True, we didn't have the mega-banks of Wall Street in ancient times, but even the bible makes mention of Bankers. And we find early methods of insurance recorded by the Babylonians in the Code of Hammurabi in 1750 B.C.

One would think that, given this much time, the industry might be able to better define and communicate the types of services available and the professionals who administer these services. The truth is that, like any other industry, there are many different players each with a different agenda. And we believe the competing agendas of these companies and professionals may have blurred the line between what services are being provided and whose interests are being served. In fact, in 2008, the United States Securities and Exchange Commission (SEC) commissioned the LRN-RAND Center for Corporate Ethics, Law, and Governance to conduct a study of the products and services provided by investment advisors and broker-dealers and evaluate investors' understanding of the differences between their products, services, duties, and obligations. The exhaustive study even looked at investors' perceptions of advisor functional and job titles. The findings were supportive of this assertion as summarized in the report: "the functional difference between investment advisers and broker-dealers has arguably become more blurred."[4]

Our goal in this section is not to give you a side-by-side comparison or review of the merits and faults of all the different types of financial firms. Instead, we share with you basic information that will help you investigate and assemble an industrious, cooperative, and competent financial planning and investing team that will meet your specific needs.

So who will you need on your team? What type of professionals will actually comprise your team? As a starting point, look at the various areas of wealth management that might apply to any sudden wealth recipient. In the following figure, a simple view of the complex wealth management process is illustrated. The wheel

---

[4] Angela K. Hung, Noreen Clancy, Jeff Dominitz, Eric Talley, Claude Berrebi, and Farrukh Suvankulov, "Investor and Industry Perspectives on Investment Advisers and Broker-Dealers" (Santa Monica, CA: RAND, 2008), 20.

consists of fourteen primary disciplines that all together make up the comprehensive wealth management process. Of course, each person's financial situation is unique. While some sudden wealth recipients may require more planning services and advisors than listed on the wheel, not everyone will have the need for an advisor from each of these disciplines.

The Wealth Wheel

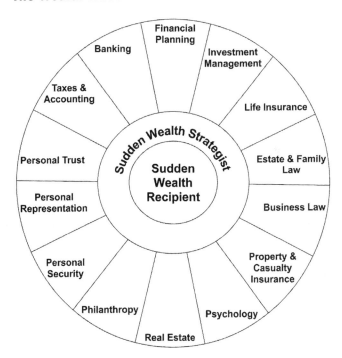

Imagine yourself at the center, or hub, of the wheel. You are the sudden wealth recipient. The spokes of the wheel list fourteen areas common to sudden wealth financial plans. Surrounding the hub is the sudden wealth strategist, who is responsible for the coordination of all the different disciplines. The strategist could be you, a friend with some financial knowledge, or a representative of any of the individual disciplines listed. However, because of the comprehensive nature of this role, the strategist's responsibilities are normally the duties of the comprehensive financial planner. Take a spin around the wheel to learn more about each of these wealth management disciplines.

Financial Planning

The impact of an unexpected financial windfall can be tremendous and either positive or negative. Decisions made early on can be vital to your success or, possibly, cause your failure. Financial choices are frequently interdependent, and sudden wealth can complicate these dependencies.

Financial planning is a comprehensive process that can help you make prudent choices. The financial planning process starts with a thorough review of your current financial situation and identification of your financial goals and potential risks. Then, a plan to achieve the goals, while addressing the risks, is developed, monitored, and adjusted over time. The Financial Planning Association provides an excellent definition of financial planning: "Financial planning is the long-term process of wisely managing your finances so you can achieve your goals and dreams, while at the same time negotiating the financial barriers that inevitably arise in every stage of life"[5].

Individuals working as financial planners are often employed by large mega-banks and insurance companies, or they may work for accounting firms or boutique wealth management firms. Some financial planning practices are operated as one-person planning firms. Choosing the right financial planner is critical to the success of your financial future.

---

5   Financial Planning Association, "What is Financial Planning?" http://www.fpanet.org/WhatisFinancialPlanning/ (accessed March 14, 2011).

While there are various credentials for financial planners, there is no single regulatory agency governing all financial planners. The following chapters will walk you through important considerations and questions to ask when selecting a planner.

Investment Management

Frequently the first specialty most sudden wealth recipients think about is the role of investment manager. The investment manager (sometimes called an asset manager) will be responsible for the day-to-day selection and oversight of stocks, bonds, and other investment options. As mentioned earlier, the varieties of investment managers are numerous and due to the sheer number of firms and specialized professional titles, the choices can be confusing. On one end of the spectrum are companies and professionals who aim to serve individuals who make their own choices of what to buy and sell. This might be your typical stockbroker, brokerage firm, or online trading firm. On the other end of the spectrum are the large national firms. While the differences between the ends of the spectrum are discernible, all the gray area between these two extremes complicates matters. In fact, if you asked a hundred professionals to define and explain the duties of an asset manager, you might get 110 different answers! When starting the search for an investment manager, ask yourself this question: How involved do I want to be in my portfolio? This includes the buys and sells, general allocation, and other tactical decisions. If you want to be actively involved in these assignments and have the time and aptitude for financial markets, then a stockbroker or online trading firm might be a good fit. If you prefer to delegate the day-to-day decisions to a professional who keeps you informed but not actively involved, then look for an advisor that can manage your account with discretion[6]. Whichever choice you make, be sure to reference the designation descriptions and review the interview questions in the following chapters.

---

6   A discretionary account is defined by the Financial Industry Regulatory Authority (FINRA) as "An account empowering a broker or adviser to buy and sell without the client's prior knowledge and consent," http://www.finra.org/Glossary/P011001.

Life Insurance

Why do I need life insurance after I just came into this windfall? You may no longer have an income replacement or debt repayment need, but you still have long-term planning needs and the responsibility to protect your money. Future estate taxes, product and tax diversification, or any number of specialized strategies fall under the category of long-term planning. Generally speaking, there are two categories of life insurance professionals: exclusive agents and independent agents or brokers. Exclusive agents represent a single life insurance company and typically can only sell products for that one company. Independent agents, on the other hand, may be contracted with many different life insurance companies. One is not necessarily better than the other; just understand that some professionals will have more product options to choose from than others.

Estate and Family Law

With sudden wealth comes more responsibility. And with more responsibility, it is imperative that you take the precautions necessary to protect your newfound wealth for your long-term needs, those of your family and possibly of your legacy or of future generations. An estate attorney is critical to better understanding and navigating the tricky maze of laws regarding property rights, taxes, wills, probate, and trusts. Some states have programs allowing attorneys to designate an estate planning specialty. Attorneys can also demonstrate their dedication to estate planning with membership to various estate planning organizations or bar associations. It is important that the lawyer you select is up-to-date with current estate tax law. Whether the attorney practices independently or in a large group, you should feel confident in their ability to answer all of your questions and handle your affairs. The office environment and level of customer service should suit your needs. That the office has a comprehensive system in place to draft and execute your plans and documents in a timely manner and to completion is important.

Business Law

Sudden wealth often opens the door to business ventures not possible without a great deal of money.

If you are considering investing or starting a private business or speculating in real estate ventures, then a business attorney will be critical to your team. Again, the choices of lawyers who specialize in business and contracts are numerous. Lawyers practicing in larger offices with many attorneys may have the ability to utilize colleagues who practice unique specialties. However, solo attorneys, through personal relationships created over the years, can have strategic alliances and capabilities with different specialty areas.

Property and Casualty Insurance

Property and casualty insurance—protection for cars, homes, boats and watercraft, fine art, jewelry, liability, and other material items—is critically important to a successful wealth management plan. Like the life insurance options, the property and casualty insurance market is composed of both, exclusive, single-company agents and brokers able to offer products from multiple companies.

Two areas of concern related to property insurance routinely surface for sudden wealth recipients.

The obvious one is the matter of the sudden wealth recipient having more, and more valuable, possessions that should be insured. Of course not all sudden wealth recipients are buying the million dollar mansions and filling their garage with expensive toys (like Nathan from Chapter 11), but more money typically translates to more possessions to protect. The second, less apparent, concern is the newfound personal liability risk. Simply stated, this is the risk that someone might sue you for whatever reason—but usually for their own financial gain. Not only is more money at stake now, some sudden wealth recipients often become more visible to the public and, as such, become a bigger target for lawsuits. Frivolous and petty litigation is rampant in the United States. Prominent physicians, property owners, or entertainers are constantly being sued for very large sums after seemingly insignificant incidents. One of the primary tenets of prudent wealth management is to protect your wealth. And a sound insurance program can play a significant role in safeguarding your new wealth.

Psychology

Sudden wealth events can be conclusions to traumatic events or sometimes joyous surprises. Yet these very different events represent similar new beginnings and an unknown financial future. Think for a moment about three individuals, each receiving a sudden windfall of $10 million—one lottery winner, one business owner, and one inheritor. Each is dealing with a myriad of conflicting emotions. The lottery winner is deliriously joyful and feeling very lucky for making—what most would consider—a foolish bet. The business owner is relieved that the work to sell a business is over but is now lost after selling the enterprise he or she devoted his or her life to over so many years. And a son is experiencing grief and overwhelming responsibility after inheriting his parents' estate. As we illustrated throughout the stories, all of these emotions and feelings can make it very difficult to move forward. Counseling can help one understand these new feelings, examine the problems and opportunities related to the sudden influx of wealth, and take action to move forward. It is considered a modern wealth management best practice for therapists to be included in a sudden wealth recipient's professional team. In fact, as the medical community continues to recognize the benefits of a healthy connection between mind and body, the financial community is increasingly aware that this holistic approach can also be applied to financial management with great results.

Real Estate

Sudden wealth may not necessitate an immediate need for a real estate professional, but as one transitions into this new stage of life, various personal, investment, and commercial real estate opportunities (or dangers!) lie in wait. Having the right real estate professional on your team means working with an individual who is not only highly competent, but also collaborative.

Real estate decisions involve large sums of money and carry a lot of legal liability. Unfortunately, it is not common for real estate professionals to be included in most integrated financial teams. But the right professional will embrace this consultative role and add value to the financial management environment. The National Association of Realtors (NAR) reports their membership at more than 1 million[7] (which doesn't include all the other real estate professionals who are not members of NAR!). So there is no shortage of options. The NAR offers several questions that are important to ask when interviewing potential agents. It's the typical list of "What's your experience?"; "What designations do you have?"; and "What marketing programs do you use?" It is also imperative to determine what business philosophy the agent follows and how he or she will work with other professionals on your financial team.

Philanthropy

Many sudden wealth recipients are inspired to support causes that are important to them at new financial levels. The most common reason cited as the primary motivation of wealthy individuals to give money to charity is simply knowing that their gift can make a difference. Of course, it is also well

---

7   National Association of Realtors, "NAR Membership," http://www.realtor.org/about_nar (accessed January 31, 2011).

known that potential income tax savings associated with charitable giving are equally important. To maximize the impact of monetary gifts, a well-designed and coordinated giving plan, as part of an overall wealth management strategy, is crucial. A solid plan should help one nurture assets and allow them to be given at the right time. Many nonprofit organizations offer planning services to assist with giving directly to them. These services can be an excellent resource; however, not all are created equal. Some financial planning firms, banks, and brokerage firms offer philanthropic services too. Keep in mind, three essential ingredients to include in your plan: support the charity you are passionate about, develop a giving plan that is sustainable and does not risk your financial well-being, and coordinate your giving plan to sync with your tax planning goals.

Personal Security

Sudden wealth and large money transactions are oftentimes public in nature, which can put the recipients at risk. Even when requested to remain private, many state lotteries can post winners' names and cities. Lawsuit settlements that end with large dollar awards are always top stories in the news. Even private estates settled through the probate process become public records. Privacy and personal security are real concerns for sudden wealth recipients.

Not everyone that receives a windfall needs to hire a personal bodyguard or station a security officer on their front lawn. But personal security is important whether it's protecting your family's e-mail and social media accounts or minimizing the risk of harm to you and your family. With the right wealth team in place before (or soon after) the sudden wealth event and using commonsense privacy safeguards, negative impacts from publicity can be minimized.

Many benefactors of a sudden financial windfall find they have no additional need for high-level security beyond what their financial and legal team provides. However, for those who find themselves in larger homes requiring more staff and outside service providers, travelling internationally (especially to exotic locales), and hosting bigger events on their property, they do have new concerns. There are numerous private security agencies for these individuals in most major cities. A financial team leader can help sort through the broad array of services including general security and bodyguard services, most personal security agencies offer.

Personal Representation

Depending on the type of sudden windfall received, one might have the need for a personal agent or representative. Obviously for athletes and entertainers, agents and representatives are responsible for the promotion of a career and for communication and negotiations with team owners and management or studios and producers.

Most sudden wealth events are not the result of a glamorous and exciting sports and entertainment contract! If you're not the next pro basketball standout, why would you need a personal representative? Simple. You may have financial tasks, both large and small, that you do not want to deal with anymore. Bill payment, shopping and other personal errands, gathering and organization of tax or medical records, real estate or property management, and meeting with contractors and designers on your remodel are all forms of personal representation. Many of these services can be handled by a private concierge firm or a personal administration practice either at your direction or at the direction of your wealth strategist. As you consider options, keep in mind, that this person or firm will act on your behalf, so choose wisely. Trust and accountability are of utmost importance.

Personal Trust

In chapter I, we saw Richard and Mary's legacy nearly squandered. Personal trusts are common tools that can help protect wealth from one generation to the next and are often used in wealth and estate planning. A properly designed trust may have helped protect Mary financially from her own decline.

A trust is a legal entity created to hold and manage assets solely for the benefit of one or more beneficiaries[8]. Trusts can be created for many purposes. For instance, some personal trusts aid in minimizing

---

8   A beneficiary is the individual or entity that is benefiting from the trust currently or that will in the future. If desired, more than one beneficiary may be named in a trust.

estate tax obligations while others ease the transfer of property to children, grandchildren, and even charitable organizations.

There are three primary services associated with personal trusts: the drafting (or creation) of the trust itself; the administration of the trust; and the management of the assets in the trust. The trust document is created by the estate planning attorney, discussed previously, while the administration and management are carried out by an individual trustee; a corporate trustee, such as a bank or trust company; or a combination of both.

A trustee accepts a great deal of responsibility in managing and administering a trust. Your choice of trustee is an important decision. Selecting an individual trustee may have the advantage of lower direct costs, personal interest in the well-being of beneficiaries, and more familiarity with your personal situation. However, before hiring an individual trustee, ensure that your choice has the appropriate experience, time, and resources to manage your trust properly. A corporate trustee can provide experience and expertise to the management and administration of trusts, however if choosing a bank or trust company be sure you understand the total costs of administration (e.g., accounting, recordkeeping, law interpretation) and asset management (e.g. management of investments, real estate, or business interests). Finally, it is important that whomever you select as trustee, he or she has the ability to manage the assets in coordination with non-trust assets.

Taxes and Accounting

It's no surprise that after experiencing a sudden wealth event, a new layer of complexity is added to annual income tax filing and planning. A highly competent and qualified accountant or Certified Public Accountant (CPA) will be needed on the team. Tax returns may no longer be simple 1040s. You will likely have multiple schedules (attachments) for new sources of income, and your short-term and long-term tax planning will need to be addressed. The largest association representing the accounting profession is the American Institute of Certified Public Accountants (AICPA). The AICPA report nearly 370,000 members across the globe[9]. Some firms are large and others are small. Find one that has the right feel for you and best answers your questions and addresses your needs. You'll also want to be sure your accountant routinely works with high-net worth individuals and has experience with sudden wealth recipients.

Banking

Regardless of how much money anyone has, a bank is required for everyday transactions. You most likely already have a bank checking account, but needs change with sudden wealth. You will still need a bank that can offer the basics, but higher balances may allow for exclusive accounts with lower fees and higher rates. You may even need specialized lending capabilities. Yes, even with a full bank account you may want to borrow money for business or real estate purposes.

Your choice could be your neighborhood bank around the corner or it could be a national mega-

---

9   American Institute o f CPAs, "About the AICPA," http://www.aicpa.org/About/Pages/About.aspx (accessed April 29, 2011).

bank. Typically small banks will offer a single point of contact but may lack the specialized rates or lending programs offered by larger banks. On the other hand, mega-banks may have every specialized product you could dream of, but you may find yourself banking through 1-800 numbers and a revolving cast of employees.

Bringing It All Together

The responsibility to coordinate this team of specialists is highly important. With several overlapping disciplines involved in making even one decision, mistakes if made, can be compounded quickly and the results can be costly. Having discussed the fourteen disciplines commonly seen in sudden wealth situations, you can see clearly that managing sudden wealth can indeed be a complex orchestration of many different advisors.

> How is a Sudden wealth Strategist similar to an Orchestra Conductor?
>
> An orchestra conductor is responsible for the orchestra preparation. He or she maintains the beat of the music, makes interpretive decisions such as the speed and intensity of passages, and communicates these decisions in rehearsal and performance. Similarly, the sudden wealth strategist prepares the financial team to develop a coordinated plan, directs the pace of implementation, and encourages effective communication between the specialists. Just as a well-conducted orchestra creates beautiful music, a well-directed financial team can compose a wonderfully orchestrated wealth plan.

The financial planner is commonly selected as the sudden wealth strategist. The Financial Planning Association's definition of a financial planner—provided earlier in this chapter—describes the multi-disciplinary nature of sudden wealth management. Financial planners are trained to be "generalists," to help identify financial issues and prepare a plan to address foreseen and unexpected issues. They are typically adept at identifying when specialists are needed and are excellent facilitators at keeping the team on track toward the goals set by the sudden wealth recipient.

It is also important to know that some advisors, based on their skills and expertise, may fill multiple roles in the wealth management process. For instance, some financial planners may offer investment management as one of their core disciplines. Or, life insurance agents may also provide philanthropic planning to clients. Multiple functions are perfectly fine. Just be sure you and your wealth strategist assign pieces of your plan according to each team member's qualifications and ability to accomplish your financial goals.

In the end, your financial team should be working together to protect, sustain, and nurture you and your wealth.

"The way a team plays as a whole determines its success. You may have the greatest bunch of individual stars in the world, but if they don't play together, the club won't be worth a dime."

Babe Ruth

FINDING YOUR TEAM COORDINATOR

"When you have to make a choice and don't make it, that is in itself a choice."

William James

When faced with a sudden wealth event, many decisions will need to be made—some later, but at least one is going to be immediate: the selection of the primary wealth strategist or financial team coordinator. This professional will help identify, prioritize, and make sense of the risks and decisions brought on by your newfound wealth. This, in turn, provides valuable time to step back, recognize and absorb the financial and emotional impacts, and ultimately ease into making the longer-term decisions at the appropriate time.

It is commonly thought that a competent and trusted financial planner makes a good choice to fill the role of sudden wealth strategist. But how do you choose the person for this important role? The title "financial planner" can be applied to just about any-one in the financial world. Bankers, insurance agents, accountants, stockbrokers, and even real estate agents sometimes call themselves financial planners.

The Financial Industry Regulatory Authority (FINRA), the largest independent regulator for all investment firms doing business in the United States, reports that there are over 630,000 registered investment professionals in the United States[10]. Life

---

10 Financial Industry Regulatory Authority, "About the Financial Industry Regulatory Authority," http://www.finra.org/AboutFINRA/ (accessed March 13, 2011).

insurance agents are licensed by individual states and many states report more than 100,000 licensed life insurance agents[11] in their state alone. Not every one of these representatives holds themselves out as an active financial planner, but the numbers shed some light on how flush the industry is with potential financial planners.

As a first step, let's consider some of the industry designations and credentials you may come across. Armed with this information, you can then begin your search by asking friends and other trusted professionals for planners they know and trust. Keep in mind this one very important fact: not all financial planners fit all situations. After creating a list of potential planners, interview them to see how they might fit into your situation.

To guide you with this important task, a list of interview questions is provided below. Along with each question, context is provided to illustrate why the question is important, what type of answers you

---

11   The National Association of Insurance Commissioners (NAIC) is an organization that coordinates and assists insurance regulators from all fifty states, the District of Columbia, and U.S. territories. To learn more about your particular state insurance department, visit its Web site at www.naic.org/state_web_map.htm.

may hear, and what it all means. These questions will help you accurately identify the right planner or firm.

The Alphabet Soup of Financial Designations

The abundance of abbreviations and acronyms for various financial professional certification programs and designations lead some to call it "financial alphabet soup". In fact, FINRA provides a reference tool that lists more than one hundred professional designations on its consumer web site[12]. This helpful tool is a great resource to find details such as experience and education requirements, exam type, and investor complaint or public disciplinary processes for each designation. FINRA does not endorse or approve any designation, nor do they imply who can or cannot use a designation. FINRA is simply providing a tool to help individuals understand some of the available financial professional designations.

With this many designations, where to start? Fortunately, there are a few primary credentials that match the duties of a wealth strategist very well. First,

---

12 http://apps.finra.org/DataDirectory/1/prodesignations.aspx

a wealth strategist needs to have a broad financial knowledge base from which to draw. Many financial designations are very specialized and while that is great for specific functions, it typically is not ideal for your financial strategist to be limited to one area of expertise. Next, the accreditation of the issuing institution or designation itself is important. Finally, we look for substantial experience and educational prerequisites, meaningful continuing education requirements, and an established investor complaint or disciplinary process.

The following credentials, listed alphabetically, fit these criteria well. Each provides a broad curriculum, is offered by an accredited educational institution, has relevant experience and educational prerequisites, requires meaningful ongoing education, and requires accountability through a consumer complaint or disciplinary process.

Certified Financial Planner (CFP®): This certification program covers major planning areas including general principles of financial planning, insurance planning and risk management, employee benefits planning, investment planning, income tax planning, retirement planning, and estate planning. It is issued by the Certified Financial Planner Board of Standards, Inc. and requires candidates to hold a bachelor's degree (or higher) and to have a minimum of three years of full-time personal financial planning experience. The candidate may sit for the certification examination after completing a board registered CFP program or another advanced degree or certification, such as a Ph.D, CFA, or attorney's license. Thirty hours of continuing education are required every two years. See www.cfp.net.

Certified Private Wealth Advisor (CPWA^{sm}): This designation program offers behavioral finance, charitable and estate planning, planning for closely held business owners, planning for executives, portfolio management, retirement planning, risk management, and tax planning. It is issued by the Investment Management Consultants Association (IMCA) and requires candidates to hold a bachelor's degree or other advanced designation, have five years of client centered experience in financial services or related industry, have an acceptable regulatory history, and receive two professional reference letters. The candidate may sit for the certification examination after completing a six-month pre-study educational program and a one-week in-class program. Forty hours of continuing education are required every two years. See www.imca.org.

Chartered Financial Consultant (ChFC®): This program covers key financial planning disciplines, including insurance, income taxation, retirement planning, investments, and estate planning. It is issued by The American College and requires candidates to have a minimum of three years of full-time business experience. The candidate may sit for the certification examination after completing six core courses and two elective courses. Thirty hours of continuing education are required every two years. See www.theamericancollege.edu.

Personal Financial Specialist (PFS): This credential is intended to develop competency in tax, estate, retirement planning, and charitable giving for CPAs. It is issued by the American Institute of Certified Public Accountants (AICPA) and requires candidates to be a CPA and member of AICPA and to have a minimum of two years of full-time personal financial planning experience. The candidate may sit for the certification examination after completing eighty hours of personal financial planning education. Sixty hours of continuing education are required every three years. See www.aicip.org.

What other designations might you run across in your search? There are a number of them, as we've said. Most are specialized to a specific discipline or product of wealth management such as, insurance, investment planning, or retirement planning. We've provided an alphabetical list of some of the more frequently seen credentials along with a basic description of the designation program below and a Web site you can visit for more information.

AAMS®—The Accredited Asset Management Specialist℠ designation is offered through the College for Financial Planning and focuses primarily on asset management, investment strategies, and investment policy development. See www.cffp.edu.

CEBS—The Certified Employee Benefit Specialist certification is a program offered by the International Foundation of Employee Benefit Plans and covers a broad array of employee benefit planning and compensation management. See www.ifebp.org.

CFA—The Chartered Financial Analyst title is offered through the CFA Institute and covers an extensive range of economics, financial analysis, investment products, and portfolio management. See www.cfainstitute.org.

CFS®—The Certified Fund Specialist® certification is offered by the Institute of Business & Finance and focuses on the analysis, selection, and use of mutual funds. See www.icfs.com.

CIMA—The Certified Investment Management Analyst program is offered through the Investment Management Consultants Association and covers a broad range of investment management topics including portfolio management, investment policy design, investment analysis, and performance measurement. See www.imca.org.

CLU®—The Chartered Life Underwriter® designation is offered through The American College to provide in-depth knowledge of the life insurance industry. See www.theamericancollege.edu.

CMFC®—The Chartered Mutual Fund Counselor^{sm} program is offered through a collaboration between the College for Financial Planning and the Investment Company Institute (ICI)—the primary trade association for the mutual fund industry. The program focuses on mutual funds, other packaged product characteristics, and application. See www.cffp.edu.

CPA—Certified Public Accountants are licensed by the licensee's State Board of Accountancy. CPAs provide accounting, tax advisory, business services, and personal financial management. See www.aicpa.org.

CRPS®—The Chartered Retirement Plan Specialist^{sm} program is offered through the College for Financial Planning and is designed to enhance the professional's knowledge of company retirement plan design, implementation, and maintenance. See www.cffp.edu

CTFA—The Certified Trust and Financial Advisor certification is maintained by the Institute of Certified Bankers and covers areas such as fiduciary and trust operations, taxes, and investment management. See www.aba.com,

Of course, many highly-qualified individuals have designations, degrees, or certificates other than those listed here. Likewise, many equally qualified individuals with no advanced degrees or certifications. So we are not saying your planner must have letters after his or her name. However, it is critical that the individual you choose as your wealth strategist has a broad financial knowledge base spanning many different wealth planning disciplines. She must also demonstrate a commitment to staying abreast of new strategies and opportunities. The pursuit and attainment of advanced financial designations and certifications indicate a level of professional competence and commitment to education.

Interview Questions

A quick online search for "questions to ask a financial planner" returns over 50,000 results. Change the search to "questions to ask a financial advisor" and the list grows to over 150,000. So what on earth could possibly be suggested in this text that is not already covered? Well, as Albert Einstein said, "Information is not knowledge."

Merriam-Webster's defines knowledge as "the fact or condition of knowing something with familiarity gained through experience or association."[13] That's what you want to learn about in your interviews – experience. Here is a list of essential questions to help sudden wealth recipients identify professionals that match their immediate and long-term financial needs. For each question, context is provided as to why it's important and how to interpret. Take notes during your interview meeting. You will likely cover a lot of material and it will be difficult to recall the details without good notes.

※ ※ ※

1. What's important for me to know about your firm?

---

13 *Merriam-Webster*, "Knowledge," http://www.merriam-webster.com/dictionary/knowledge (accessed March 9, 2011).

Now you can ask the potential planner about his practice. You will want to know what services he offers, how many clients he personally services, and what his typical client profile looks like. What you are trying to determine with this question is if the goals of this practice are a good match to you and your needs. If an individual planner brags about "hundreds" of clients, it might be an indication that you won't get very personalized service. Plus, you are interviewing a planner to be your team coordinator, or "quarterback," and for him to provide the depth of holistic service this entails, it will take quite a bit of personal attention and time. And there are only so many hours in a day!

2. Have you had clients in similar situations to mine?

Do not make the mistake of assuming that the age of your potential planner means she is experienced. The industry if filled with "aged" rookies. You also do not want to be the first sudden wealth client for your new planner. And be specific. For instance, if you are a lottery winner, ask if your interviewee has worked with any lottery winners. If you determine that she is a seasoned professional with cases like yours, probe a little deeper. Ask what these plans and engagements typically look like. This will give you a good idea if she is willing to be (or capable of being) your team coordinator.

3. What licenses, designations, and credentials do you maintain?

You'll likely see some credentials on the planner's business card, but ask the planner to discuss her industry licenses too (those required by state and federal regulatory agencies). This will give you an idea if the planner is able to work with both investment and insurance products, or just one. Specifically, you will want to know when she obtained a license, what it is, and why she holds the license. Finally ask if the planner has ever been disciplined by any government or professional regulatory authority.

4. How is your firm organized?

With this question, you are trying to learn whose interests your potential planner needs to serve and what support and resources are available for your planner. If the planner's practice is independently owned, ask how they handle compliance and oversight (in other words, who's looking over their shoulder). You do not want your planner's brother keeping an eye on their operations!

You want a firm with an established operations and technology platform. Operations include areas such as account opening, trade processing, and legal and compliance. Technology provides systems for online account management, statement and performance reporting, and planning and trading systems.

If the planner is with a major firm, find out if they have sales or "production" goals. Also, ask if the planner's firm produces any investment or insurance product. If they do, then the planner is considered part of their distribution force and may be expected to sell a certain amount of their products.

5. What is your financial planning philosophy? And how will this influence your development of a plan for me?

You've made it through the more technical questions, and now you are trying to learn how this planner approaches financial risks and opportunities. Try to determine if she is a risk taker or a steady mover. Also, as you listen to the response to this question, remember that financial planning is not a product; it is an ongoing service. So if the planner seems more interested in talking about a deliverable (i.e., a leather-bound notebook with two hundred pages!), you might want to ask a few more questions about how she monitors your progress with the plan execution and adjust to changes in your life, the markets, and the economy. There's nothing wrong with a fancy binder, but remember that a wealth plan is a living plan that will change over time. You are looking for a long-term relationship.

6. How do you see us working together?

This question may have been answered for you by now, but if not, it is important to ask. Remember, you are interviewing the professional sitting in front of you to be your personal financial team coordinator. You don't want someone that will just sit back and take orders from you and other team members. Of course, you want someone who will be cooperative, but you need a leader who is willing and able to effectively guide you and the team toward your goals.

7. How and in what ways will my plan be implemented?

This is possibly the most overlooked question we have seen. As the old saying goes, "plan your work and work your plan." What good is a plan if you do not follow through with it? Who is going to take the responsibility that your plan is developed and implemented? It should be the person you hire to create it—that's what you are paying for isn't it? This does not mean your planner has to personally execute a trade, draft a document, or transfer title to a trust. It does mean that the planner is continually asking and reminding you or whichever team specialist it is, to complete the task.

8. Who specifically will I work with at your firm?

This planner (and his or her firm) is being interviewed to potentially be your financial team lead. It is important to understand how involved this individual will be in your planning issues. Who will be your day-to-day client service contact? Will your planner pass your file off to a junior planner or to a back-office financial planning division? Will you have a joint relationship with multiple professionals in the office or one point of contact? Technically, there is no right or wrong answer here. However, we would suggest that having a senior or lead planner personally draft your recommendations tends to create more buy in and commitment to ensure the plan is executed and implemented properly. At the end of the day, just be sure you understand who is doing what on your team.

9. How do you charge for your services?

Fill a room full of planners and ask this question, stand back and watch the room divide. Why is this such a charged question? Let's start with a bit of background.

There are three primary ways planners can be compensated for their services: fee only, fee based, and commission. Fee only means they charge either an hourly rate or flat fee to develop a plan or counsel you on a situation. Fee based typically means the planner charges a set percentage on the assets she manages and has the ability to utilize products that pay a commission. Commission means that the planner is paid by a product sponsor for selling one of its products. We have purposely left salary and salary/bonus off the list because these terms do not relate to how you, the client, pays; it is simply how the planner is paid by the firm.

So which is better? We suggest there is not one right answer. Through our years in the industry, we have seen good advisors using each of the methods and we have seen bad advisors using each of the methods. What we've come to realize is that how an advisor generates revenue is not as important as how he or she chooses to disclose the compensation.

To be completely objective, and have the ability to utilize all available products or strategies, she will need to be able to provide fee-based services and commissionable products. For instance, imagine the situation where a fee-only planner determines that a commissionable insurance product is the best option for a particular client. If he or she cannot sell insurance, the planner will need to refer the client to an insurance agent. The agent may or may not have the client's best interests at heart.

Now that you understand the differences of these fee structures, you should determine how much your potential planner usually charges for cases similar to yours.

10. How much do you typically charge for your services?

If the planner is a fee-only or fee-based planner, find out what the hourly rate or engagement fee is and get an estimate of the total cost in dollars. Realize that at this early stage, the planner will not be able to give you an exact dollar cost, but get a copy of the fee schedule and an estimate in writing. If the planner intends to charge an asset management fee, ask for the fee schedule and determine which assets will be included in the fee. For commission-based planners, ask what the typical commission percentage is on the products they sell and find out if they receive any other compensation in the form of trips, prizes, or other incentives from the product provider.

11. How often will we meet?

Expect to have a few more meetings early on in the relationship. You will likely be reviewing new account documents and financial planning drafts more frequently the first few months. Plus your planner will likely be coordinating necessary meetings with bankers, tax and legal advisors, and other team specialists, as needed. After things settle down, expect no less than two or three meetings per year.

12. How do you structure and organize your client review meetings?

Early meetings will be focused on determining what is important to you and your family and what immediate actions are necessary with your windfall. After the first year or so, your plan should be running smoothly so expect the typical investment performance updates and continued planning meetings to start work on your intermediate and longer-term actions.

13. Can you provide any references?

In addition to the individual that referred you in the first place, ask for two or three references. Ideally the references will be from people with situations similar to yours. Be prepared to share some basic information about your situation to the reference. They will be concerned about their privacy as much as you are. Since the prospective planner will obviously provide you with individuals who think positively of the planner and the firm, be prepared to ask the reference some direct questions.

Ask what types of services the planner provides for them and how long they have worked with the planner. Ask how the planner handles and interacts with other team professionals. For instance, for the

CPA or the attorney, ask if the fee arrangements have been easy to understand and are going according to plan. Find out how easy the advisor is to contact and how frequently they communicate. Finally ask what the three "best" things this advisor has done for them are.

* * *

After asking all of these interview questions, your note pages should be pretty full. Take a moment to review your notes, and clarify with your potential planner any missing pieces of information. There is no need to hire the planner on the spot. Take some time after the meeting to reflect on the specific answers to your questions and your general feeling or comfort level during the meeting.

Ask yourself these questions: How interested was the potential planner in me? And, what questions did he or she ask of me? Believe it or not, the best planners will also be interviewing you in the interview meeting to determine if you would be a good fit for their practice or not. If the potential planner did not ask you many questions, maybe he or she is more interested in pitching services than determining if he or she can be of value to you as your wealth strategist.

Be sure to call and speak with the references you obtained. And finally, head to your computer and verify the regulatory and disciplinary information you obtained in the interview meeting. To check the disciplinary history of the planner, visit the following regulatory agencies' Web sites:

- **Financial Industry Regulatory Authority:** FINRA BrokerCheck® is a free tool to help investors research the professional backgrounds of current and former FINRA registered brokerage firms and brokers. Visit the Web site athttp://brokercheck.finra.org/
- **U.S. Securities and Exchange Commission:** The SEC provides several tools you can use to check the regulatory status of brokers, investment advisors, and their firms. See www.sec.gov

- **National Association of Insurance Commissioners:** Your state insurance commission will have status of your advisor's insurance licenses, if any. To find a listing of state insurance commissions, visit NAIC's website. www.naic.org
- **Certified Financial Planner Board of Standards, Inc.:** If your prospective planner is a CFP® professional, check his or her disciplinary status at its Web site: www.cfp.net/search/

As important as this decision is to make, it is important that you ask the appropriate questions. It happens far too often that an individual going through a significant financial life transition avoids this important first step and suffers needlessly years later.

As you go on your search for your team coordinator or wealth strategist, we offer these words of encouragement. There are plenty of educated, ethical, and experienced advisors available. Pay attention to your emotions as you listen to planners answer these questions. If you do, you will be well prepared to make this important decision.

> "Life is the sum of all your choices."
>
> *Albert Camus*

PREPARING FOR YOUR FIRST MEETING

"All we want are the facts, ma'am."

Sgt. Joe Friday

Congratulations! You've selected the professional or firm that will take on the role of sudden wealth strategist. That is a big step and hopefully you are already feeling a bit of relief. Now is the point in time that you will need to begin gathering documents and information for your planner.

Your strategist will have a lot of questions for you as they develop your wealth profile. Some planners may use a detailed paper questionnaire or online data gathering tool. No matter how the information is collected, the content of the information is generally the same. We've provided a sample of a data gathering form that would be typical from a comprehensive wealth management/planning firm.

Remember that the detail of the questions is not just for the sake of curiosity! In reality, the more information your planner has about you, your family, your experiences with money, your financial fears and concerns, and your future monetary needs, wants, and wishes, the better job he or she can do at helping you develop an integrated and actionable plan. So, answer honestly and completely!

Personal History

Your planner will need to know basic personal and family information. Of course this would include your name, address, and contact details; but your full history will include more personal questions such as date of birth, Social Security Number, possibly personal health information, and names of your children, grandchildren, other dependents.

Financial Documents

As your planner helps you build a wealth plan, she will need to examine your current financial documents. Some of the most commonly requested documents are

- Account statements including, bank accounts, investment accounts, retirement accounts, deferred compensation, personal trust, and other financial accounts.
- Life insurance policies and the latest annual statements along with any current insurance proposals.
- Disability and long-term care insurance policies, including benefit details.

- Business ownership documents such as partnership agreements, buy–sell agreements, and business financial statements.
- Current estate-planning documents including your will, power of attorney, and any trust agreements.
- Latest personal income tax return including schedules and worksheets.
- Current income detail, such as annual salary and bonus or social security and pension payments.
- Future income projections including Social Security and pension estimates.

Planning Priorities and Goals

Sudden wealth has its own unique sets of financial and life planning goals. However, the typical set of wealth planning goals will, at some point, be integrated into your personal plan. The process of identifying these immediate and long-term goals is always a thought-provoking exercise. Don't expect to know immediately what these are. Your planner should coach you through the process, and it typically develops over an extended time. The typical financial categories addressed in wealth planning are

- Portfolio management.
- Income tax efficiency.
- Major purchases.
- Education planning for children and other family members.
- Retirement savings and accumulation.
- Retirement income and distribution.
- Current or expected business sales.
- Family protection in the event of premature death, disability, or long-term care.
- Asset protection and risk management.
- Estate planning (for taxes, distribution, equalization, and legacy).
- Current and planned giving.
- Special needs.

Financial Statement and Inventory Worksheets

With the proliferation of personal finance software, many individuals can quickly print a net-worth statement or current balance sheet that lists your financial account balances. However, as you are planning to meet with your wealth team members, they may ask for more information than a simple listing of what you own and how much you owe the bank. Remember, your wealth team is not only assessing where you are financially today but is also looking for areas of risk and exposure to your current wealth. Some examples of information your planner will be looking for that are not readily apparent from your net-worth statement could include the following: Are your assets titled (or owned) by you individually, or jointly with your husband? Does your business ownership expose you to unexpected personal liability? Is your new windfall at risk of being depleted prematurely due to extended long-term care expenses? Are your charitable gifts in line with your legacy goals? These questions, and more, are all potentially important to your long-term wealth preservation and growth plans, so take them seriously and help your planner gather the appropriate information. The following financial inventory worksheets will help you prepare for your planning meetings.

Simplified Personal Financial Statement

Use the following sections to list your assets and liabilities. Indicate whether each asset is titled separately in the name of you, your spouse, jointly, or in another entity such as a Trust, LLC, or Partnership. And list the creditor for each of your loans.

Cash and Investment Assets—Be sure to list checking and savings accounts, CDs, investment account, 401(k), annuities and IRAs.

Asset Description	Owned by	Value
_____	_____	$ _____
_____	_____	$ _____
_____	_____	$ _____
_____	_____	$ _____
_____	_____	$ _____

Personal and Business Assets—This section will include items such as your home, vacation home, automobiles, furnishings, RVs or watercraft, collectibles, business interests, and any other physical assets.

Asset Description	Owned by	Value
_____	_____	$ _____
_____	_____	$ _____
_____	_____	$ _____
_____	_____	$ _____
_____	_____	$ _____

Liabilities—Loans due from you should be listed here. Include items such as your mortgage, car loans, student loans, credit card debt, business loans you are personally liable for, and other loans.

Asset Description	Obligation of	Value
_____	_____	$ _____
_____	_____	$ _____
_____	_____	$ _____
_____	_____	$ _____
_____	_____	$ _____

Household Income and Spending Plan

The spending plan is a great resource to help you identify where your money goes on a monthly basis. It's like a budget, but is not necessarily meant to control your family's monthly spending. Use the table below to detail your household income and identify your major areas of spending.

INCOME	MONTHLY	ANNUAL
Your Salary and Bonus or 1099 Income	$ _____	$ _____
Spouse's Salary and Bonus or 1099 Income	$ _____	$ _____
Investment Income (dividends and interest)	$ _____	$ _____
Rental or Other Commercial Income	$ _____	$ _____

	MONTHLY	ANNUAL
Social Security, Pension, Alimony, or Other Income	$	$
Total Income =	$	
SPENDING	**MONTHLY**	**ANNUAL**
Housing (mortgage, rent)	$	$
Property Insurance and Taxes	$	$
Utilities, Association Fees, Maintenance	$	$
Mortgage, Equity, and Other Loans	$	$
Vehicle Insurance, Taxes, Maintenance, and Other	$	$
Food and Groceries	$	$
Clothing and Personal Care	$	$
Child Care, Support, Education, Activities	$	$
Mobile Phone Plans	$	$
Dining, Entertainment, and Recreation	$	$
Vacation and Travel	$	$
Health care (medical, prescription, dental)	$	$
Medical Insurance Premiums	$	$
Life, Disability, and Long-term Care Insurance Premiums	$	$

Excess Liability Insurance Premiums	$ _____	$ _____
Other Expenses Not Listed	$ _____	$ _____
Total Spending =	$ _____	$ _____
Total Income	$ _____	$ _____
Less Total Spending	$ _____	$ _____
HOUSEHOLD INCOME SURPLUS OR (SHORTFALL) =	$ _____	$ _____

Financial Inventory Worksheet

The categories below ask for information beyond what is typically gathered from financial statements and spending plans. Provide as much detail as you can so that an accurate assessment can be made.

Life Insurance Inventory—List each policy description, death benefit, type of policy, year purchased, owner, insured, beneficiary, cash value, loans, and original purpose of policy.

_____
_____
_____
_____

*Name of Life Insurance Agent:*_____

Disability Insurance Inventory—List each policy description, insured, tax status, short-term and long-term benefit, elimination period and duration.

_____

*Name of Disability Insurance Agent:*_____

Long-Term Care Insurance Inventory - List each policy description, insured benefit amount and period, elimination period, and inflation option.

_____

_____

*Name of Long-Term Care Insurance Agent:*_____

Property & Excess Liability Insurance Summary—Provide information about your primary home (size, age, type, etc.), autos, including drivers and ages, and any valuables, such as antiques, jewelry, or collectibles. List any additional real estate, watercraft, aircraft, or recreational vehicles owned.

_____

_____

_____

*Name of Property Insurance Agent:*_____

Estate Planning & Tax Worksheet

The categories below ask for information beyond what is typically gathered from financial statements and spending plans. Provide as much detail as you can so that an accurate assessment can be made.

Name of Estate Planning Attorney:_____

Date of last formal estate planreview (or date of will execution):_____

For any revocable or irrevocable trusts created, list the grantor, trustee, beneficiaries, and date of execution and funding:

_____

If you have made any prior estate planning gifts, list the beneficiary name, amount and date of gifts:

_____

For each retirement plan/account or life insurance policy, list the primary and contingent beneficiaries (include % if more than one):

_____

_____

Tax Information

Name of CPA or Tax Advisor:_____

What is your current and future (expected) income tax rate?_____

If you have any capital loss carryovers, please list:

If you have you or your spouse used any lifetime gift or generation skipping exemption amount, provide amount:

PREPARING YOUR LOVED ONES

"Other things may change us, but we start and end with family."

Anthony Brandt

We introduced the process of estate planning in chapter 17 and the importance of estate planning is found throughout the stories in this book. Perhaps the most poignant discussion of the pitfalls of not planning was the story of Mary and Richard in chapter 1.

Recall the troubling situation in which Mary and Richard's family found themselves after Richard's unexpected death. The family experienced an emotional journey from joy, to shock, to confusion, to sorrow.

Like many families experiencing similar situations, they took each day, one-by-one. They leaned on each other for support and looked to fill in the holes of a plan that were never fully addressed. Unexpected death and incapacity can leave a family struggling. And the result can be both emotionally and financially devastating to the family. It did not need to be so difficult for Mary and Richard's family.

What can you do now to help your loved ones when one of these situations arises? First and foremost, don't be afraid to plan. We promise that planning for these events will not tempt fate. In fact, you will likely find the process both comforting and fulfilling. The information in this chapter will get you started.

Before you begin, however, ask yourself two questions: "What do I want for my loved ones and myself if I become incapacitated?" and "What do I want for my loved ones when I am gone?" The answers to these questions will keep you on the right path when developing your plan.

There are two key components of an effective estate plan. The first component, of course, is the formal process of creating wills, trusts, and other estate documents. The other, often overlooked, component is a simple (yet important) statement of wishes regarding how you would like your affairs to be carried out at your death or if you become incapacitated.

Formal Estate Planning Process

The formal process involves the development of strategy, drafting, and execution of your estate planning documents. Together, your wealth planning team will help you clarify your plan. Your estate planning attorney will be responsible for the actual creation of the documents.

In addition to the financial detail gathered by your wealth strategist, you will need to start thinking about qualitative factors. For instance, "Who would you want to administer your estate?"; "Who would be a good guardian for your kids?"; "Would you prefer a corporate trustee or individual?"; and "Who would make decisions for you if you were to become incapacitated?"

After your strategy is designed, and the documents are completed and executed, your sudden wealth strategist, your attorney, and other relevant specialists will help you implement the plan appropriately. This may include establishing new bank or investment accounts, transferring property, changing the beneficiaries of insurance policies or retirement accounts, re-titling property, or changing account ownership types.

Statement of Wishes

The emotional toll of death or incapacity of a loved one can make it very difficult to make basic decisions. You can help your loved ones through this difficult period by creating a document that can be used by your loved ones as a handbook that provides clarification of your wishes and desires upon your incapacity or eventual death. While not replacing any term or provision in your will or other formal estate planning documents, it can be an invaluable aid for your loved ones when the time arises.

A Statement of Wishes is typically written in the form of a letter, using everyday language, directly to those that will be responsible for your affairs at some point in time. Use the template in this chapter as a guide to draft your personal letter to your family and loved ones.

SUDDEN WEALTH... Blessing *or* Burden?

From: _____
Date Prepared: _____
Date(s) Reviewed: _____
　　　　　　　　　_____
　　　　　　　　　_____

Dear Family:

I have written this letter to help you through a difficult time. The instructions in this letter represent my wishes and beliefs in the event of my incapacity and/or passing. Please follow these instructions to the best of your ability. It is not my intent to alter any provision of my will; therefore, if any of these instructions differ from the provisions in my estate-planning documents, the provisions of my will or other estate-planning documents shall control.

I have also included important information regarding my advisors, financial documents, accounts, and property.

Emergency Contacts

Name _____ Phone _____
　Relationship _____
Name _____ Phone _____
　Relationship _____
Name _____ Phone _____
　Relationship _____

Advisors and Important Contacts - List the Name, Phone Number, and E-mail address for each of the following.

Financial Professional _____
Estate Planning Attorney _____
CPA/Accountant _____
Business Attorney _____
Life Insurance Agent _____
Auto & Home Insurance Agent _____

Banker _____
Primary Care Physician _____
Employer (or Former Employer) _____
Other(s) _____

Financial Assets - List details of each account owned, such as checking, savings, Brokerage, IRA, 529, etc.

Bank Name_____
   Contact _____ Phone _____ E-mail _____
   Account # _____ Type _____
   Typical Balance $ _____ Purpose _____

   Account # _____ Type _____
   Typical Balance $ _____ Purpose _____

   Account # _____ Type _____
   Typical Balance $ _____ Purpose _____

Bank Name_____
   Contact _____ Phone _____ E-mail _____
   Account # _____ Type _____
   Typical Balance $ _____ Purpose _____

   Account # _____ Type _____
   Typical Balance $ _____ Purpose _____

   Account # _____ Type _____
   Typical Balance $ _____ Purpose _____

My investment decisions are influenced by the following guiding principles._____
_____

As a matter of principle, I avoid the following types of investments. _____
_____

Investment Firm _____
  Contact _____ Phone _____ E-mail _____
  Account # _____ Type _____
  Balance $ _____ Purpose _____
  Account # _____ Type _____
  Balance $ _____ Purpose _____
  Account # _____ Type _____
  Balance $ _____ Purpose _____

Investment Firm _____
  Contact _____ Phone _____ E-mail _____
  Account # _____ Type _____
  Balance $ _____ Purpose _____
  Account # _____ Type _____
  Balance $ _____ Purpose _____
  Account # _____ Type _____
  Balance $ _____ Purpose _____

Annuity Contract # _____ Firm _____ Balance $ _____
  Contact _____ Phone _____ E-mail _____
Annuity Contract # _____ Firm _____ Balance $ _____
  Contact _____ Phone _____ E-mail _____
Annuity Contract # _____ Firm _____ Balance $ _____
  Contact _____ Phone _____ E-mail _____

Cash on Hand (amount, where located): _____

Stock and Bond Certificates on Hand

(Name, # of Shares/Face Amount, Tax Basis, Market Value, Where Located)

_____
_____
_____
_____

Life Insurance

Company _____ Phone _____ Date Issued _____
  Policy # _____ Face Amount $ _____ Cash Value $ _____
  Insured_____Beneficiary_____Owner _____
  Included Riders (disability, LTC, etc.) _____
  Location of Policy and Comments _____

Company _____ Phone _____ Date Issued _____
  Policy # _____ Face Amount $ _____ Cash Value $ _____
  Insured_____Beneficiary_____Owner _____
  Included Riders (disability, LTC, etc.) _____
  Location of Policy and Comments _____

Company _____ Phone _____ Date Issued _____
  Policy # _____ Face Amount $ _____ Cash Value $ _____
  Insured_____Beneficiary_____Owner _____
  Included Riders (disability, LTC, etc.) _____
  Location of Policy and Comments _____

Company _____ Phone _____ Date Issued _____
  Policy # _____ Face Amount $ _____ Cash Value $ _____
  Insured_____Beneficiary_____Owner _____
  Included Riders (disability, LTC, etc.) _____
  Location of Policy and Comments _____

Disability Insurance

Company_____ Payor _____
  Policy # _____ Premium $ _____ Annual Benefit $ _____
  Location of Policy and Comments _____

SUDDEN WEALTH... Blessing *or* Burden?

Long-term Care Insurance
Company_____ Payor _____
   Policy # _____ Premium $ _____ Annual Benefit $ _____
   Location of Policy and Comments _____

Health Insurance
Company_____ Payor _____
   Policy # _____ Premium $ _____ Annual Benefit $ _____
   Location of Policy and Comments _____
Medicare/Medigap Type _____
   Policy # _____ Location of Documents _____
Prescription Plan Carrier _____
   Policy # _____ Location of Documents _____

Auto, Home, Property Insurance
Company Name _____
   Contact _____ Phone _____ E-mail _____
   Policy # _____ Annual Premium $ _____ Type of Coverage __
   Policy # _____ Annual Premium $ _____ Type of Coverage __
   Policy # _____ Annual Premium $ _____ Type of Coverage __
   Location of Policies and Comments: _____

Company Name _____
   Contact _____ Phone _____ E-mail _____
   Policy # _____ Annual Premium $ _____ Type of Coverage __
   Policy # _____ Annual Premium $ _____ Type of Coverage __
   Policy # _____ Annual Premium $ _____ Type of Coverage __
   Location of Policies and Comments: _____

Other Insurance
   Details: _____
_____
_____

Other Assets—List pertinent details and locations of documents, as necessary.

Note Receivable _____

Deferred Compensation _____

Business Interests _____

Motor Vehicle Information _____

_____

Property in Storage _____

Loaned Property _____

Safe Deposit Boxes: _____

Personal Safe Location/Combination _____

Frequent Flyer Miles/Cash Back cards _____

Collectibles, Jewelry, Photographs, Heirlooms, etc. _____

_____

Medical Storage (cord blood, stem cell, embryo) _____

Other _____

_____

Real Estate—Provide details of property, mortgage, purchase date, and basis, as necessary.

Primary Home _____

Other R/E _____

_____

_____

Liabilities—List lender, amounts, payment, balance, and locations of documents, as necessary.

Loan _____

Loan _____

Credit Card _____

Credit Card _____

Leases _____

Personal Guarantees _____

I have the following ongoing financial responsibilities that I wish to continue. _____
_____

I am involved in the following lawsuit(s). _____

Income Sources—List details of any current or expected income sources.
Social Security _____
Company Pension _____
Income Annuities _____

_____
Military/VA benefits _____
Trust Beneficiary _____
Inheritance _____

Documents and Locations—Provide date signed and location of the following documents.
Unless otherwise indicated, the typical location of my important stored records is _____
_____

Will _____
Trusts, Partnership Agreements _____
General Power of Attorney _____
Medical Power of Attorney _____
Living Will _____
Other Estate Documents _____
Social Security Card _____
Drivers License _____
Birth Certificates/Adoption Papers _____
Marriage/Divorce Documents _____
Passports _____
Prepaid Funeral Contracts _____
Military Papers _____
Employment Papers _____

Tax Returns _____

Special Notes upon My Incapacitation
My general feeling of nursing home versus. home health care is _____
_____

My general beliefs and comments related to long-term care are _____
_____

Other information I think is important to consider if I become incapacitated _____
_____
_____

Special Notes upon My Death
Please notify the following family, friends and organizations of my passing _____
_____
_____

My final wishes are _____
_____
_____

I would like to have my obituary placed in the following newspapers, newsletters, etc. _____
_____
_____

Information for My Obituary
My Date and Place of Birth _____
My Spouse _____
My Children and Grandchildren _____
My Parents and Siblings _____
_____

SUDDEN WEALTH... Blessing *or* Burden?

My Relatives _____
Schools attended, dates of graduations, degrees, honors, etc. _____
_____
_____

Military Service _____
Other information for my obituary _____
_____
_____

Home/Crematory
I have already made preneed arrangements with the following funeral home/crematory _____
_____

I do not have preneed arrangements, but would prefer that you use the following funeral home/crematory _____
_____

Funeral Home/ Crematory Instructions
I would like to have a (circle all that apply): Funeral Service; Memorial Service; with Remains Present/Not Present; Open Casket; Closed Casket
I do not want a service, but prefer (circle preference) direct burial; cremation.
I would like my funeral/memorial service to be held at the following facility _____
_____

Minister, Rabbi, Individual to perform my service _____
_____

Individual(s) to give my eulogy, homily or words of comfort at my service _____
_____
_____

Music, Poetry, Readings, and Scripture Selections _____
_____

Flower Preference _____

I would like to wear the following clothing _____
I would like these individuals to be Pallbearers _____

I would like these individuals to be Flower bearers _____

In lieu of flowers, please ask for donations to _____

Burial/Entombment/Inurnment
Final disposition to be made at _____
I have already purchased a burial plot/mausoleum/crypt/cremation niche at _____

I would like my burial plot/mausoleum/crypt/cremation niche to be near the following individual

Other _____

Headstone/Casket Selection
I would like my headstone to be designed as follows (color, shape, size, flowers, emblems, etc.)

I would like my headstone to be engraved as follows _____

I would like my casket to be (metallic, wood, color, etc.) _____

Other headstone/casket selection instructions _____

Distribution of Personal Property
I request that the following personal property be distributed to the following beneficiaries in the event of my death (property description, beneficiary)

SUDDEN WEALTH... Blessing *or* Burden?

_____
_____
_____
_____
_____
_____
_____

Special Requests:

_____
_____
_____

With much love,

A LOOK INSIDE ESTATE SETTLEMENT AND PROBATE

"Never say you know a man until you have divided an inheritance with him."

Johann Kaspar Lavater

Of the many types of sudden wealth events, possibly the one most embroiled by challenges is inheritance. Consider the array of challenges facing an inheritor — the immediate question of "what do I do now?", the legal hurdles and administrative issues of estate settlement, the deadlines and timeframes, the family disputes, and all of this while you're consumed with grief.

Through the years, we've heard and witnessed all sorts of experiences surrounding inheritors and executors. And, as mentioned previously, in cases that progress and finalize smoothly, the common denominator is frequently a well-designed and drafted estate plan that includes open communication and direction to those left behind. We've outlined a critical supplement to the formal estate planning process — the Statement of Wishes — this letter can act as a crucial guide in helping your loved ones understand your choices and simplify the decisions they will be making in the months and years ahead.

But what do you do if your benefactors left no such guide? What if they have the proper legal documents in place, but never communicated the 'how's and why's? Or worse, what if no planning has been done at all? These are just some of the questions we've received from readers of the previous edition of this book, so we thought a chapter that explored this topic in more detail was necessary. Of course, one of the major challenges in tackling this subject is that each state, and even county, can have different laws and processes directing the estate administration process. As mentioned earlier, an Estate Planning Attorney experienced in your state will be a critical member of your wealth team as you proceed through the probate and administration process. Your attorney will be able to guide you properly through the legal steps necessary. Obviously all estates are not created equally and those involved will be making very unique and personal decisions.

There are many excellent guides that detail the steps involved for your particular state. In fact, some probate courts even provide written guidance specific to your state and county procedures. You may also have friends that have been through this life transition and heard their stories—both good and bad.

Throughout this text, we've discussed the importance of an experienced team to help you work through your specific estate settlement process. With that in mind, we would like to provide you with an outline of one family's journey through estate settlement to give you a preview of what you might expect in your journey.

Let's begin with some basic terminology. The term "probate" refers to the act of validating or proving a will before a court. Frequently "probate" is used informally to reference all the steps in the estate settlement process. The individual responsible for the estate administration is the "executor." The executor is named in the deceased's will and as an inheritor you may or may not be the executor of the estate. We'll discuss circumstances facing both the executor inheritor, and the non-executor inheritor with the following case involving Sylvia and her brother Robert following the death of their mother, Sonya.

Background

Sonya, the family matriarch, amassed a small fortune with her husband throughout the 1950s on their West Texas ranch. As Ms. Sonya would say, "The cattle business was just fine. But the oil business – well that was a whole new ballgame!" Sonya and Robert Sr. sold the ranch in the 1980s. Sonya was widowed in 2005. Their estate at the time was valued around $11 million. Fortunately, after selling the ranch, Sonya and Robert Sr. executed a basic estate plan. The plan had all the usual documents, general powers of attorney, medical directives, a bypass trust, and of course, their wills. When Robert Sr. passed away, estate settlement was straightforward, with their attorney and local bank handling the majority of all necessary actions. Sonya and the kids didn't have much to do except organize the funeral and sign some papers. Sonya, in her 84 year-old, strong West Texas way, bounced back quickly and continued to enjoy time with her children and grandchildren. That was until after a brief battle with cancer, she passed away at age 87.

Immediate Steps

Robert Jr., still living in the same town as Sonya, took the reins and contacted the funeral home they used for his father's funeral a few years prior.

He scheduled a meeting with a funeral director, allowing enough time for Sylvia to fly in from Alabama.

When Sylvia arrived, they went by mom's home to look for her will and any other documents they "thought would be important." The home was neat and tidy, but the closets were filled with boxes of old papers and files. They finally came across the will and other estate planning documents tucked away in a leather binder in a bookshelf with family photo albums.

A quick glance through the documents revealed that Sylvia was named as the executor to Sonya's estate and the successor trustee to the trust created when Robert Sr. passed away. Sonya had not mentioned these responsibilities to either of her kids. They both had assumed that Robert, being the son and living in the same town, would have been named. But they were okay with the decision, as they get along very well.

The meeting with the funeral director went well. The director had many questions, but also provided tremendous assistance. She informed Sylvia and Robert that their mother purchased her burial plot at a local cemetery next to Robert Sr. at the time of his death. She also had selected the grave marker and had her name and birth date engraved. She did not select a casket, nor had she pre-arranged for her services. It's important to note that many times heirs find their deceased loved ones either prepaid for their funeral services or purchased burial insurance. Before signing funeral contracts, double check with the funeral home and locate any documents to help determine if any pre-planning has been done.

With the director's guidance, the plan quickly fell in to place. Sylvia and Robert had to make several decisions such as the type of casket, the type of service, the music to be played, how large the attendance might be, do they want the premium thank you card kit or the basic kit, and even if they wanted limousine service provided. They were also responsible for writing the obituary, however the funeral home offered to submit the obituary to the local newspaper and other media outlets. The director placed the orders for death certificates.

It's a good idea to order at least ten copies as official copies will generally be needed when filing the

Federal Estate Tax Return, closing bank and investment accounts, terminating service contracts, filing for insurance benefits, and any number of other transactions. Of course additional copies can be ordered after the fact, but it's better to be prepared in advance.

The following day, Sylvia and Robert began contacting family and friends. They were surprised to hear how quickly the news was spreading. Sonya's church already had a group in place to help the family deal with the basics of organizing a reception and providing meals to the family to take some of the burden off their shoulders.

It is important to keep a journal of all gifts, flowers, meals, and any other form of assistance. It can be difficult to remember all the acts of kindness that friends and family provide to you during this time, and without a record, thank you cards will be difficult, if not impossible, to send.

Let Estate Settlement Begin

After the flurry of activity surrounding the funeral passed, it was time to start the estate settlement process. Unfortunately, the attorney that drafted Sonya's last will was no longer practicing law, however, Sonya's banker was able to recommend another attorney in town. Sylvia promptly scheduled a meeting with the new attorney to review her mother's documents and determine the plan. The attorney requested that Sylvia bring to the meeting copies of bank, investment, and retirement account statements, life insurance policies, pension and annuity statements, real estate records, and her last income tax return. Easier said than done! Past tax returns were in a box in the guest room closet, an insurance policy and real estate deed were found in a file box under the bed, and recent statements were piled in the roll top desk in her room.

The attorney helped Sylvia and Robert sort through these documents and compile a snapshot of Sonya's estate. They knew mom and dad did well with the ranch, but they were a little surprised to see it all in black and white. Sonya's bank and investment accounts alone totaled more than $2 million and she had trust accounts valued over $8 million. Indeed, Sonya's estate was of sufficient size to require a Federal Estate Tax return and the attorney suggested a CPA experienced with estate tax filings.

As executor of the estate, Sylvia along with her attorney would need to appear before the local probate judge. The attorney's office took care of all the paperwork with the court and scheduled the hearing. After the will was accepted for probate, the court provided Sylvia with the relevant documents giving her the authority to act on behalf of the estate.

Then the work started to pile up. Below is a summary of the to-do list Sylvia's attorney helped her create along with important comments and suggestions:

Notifications

- Contact creditors and publish a notice to file claim.
- Contact the Social Security Office and Medicare. Most funeral homes notify the Social Security Office; however it is a good idea to contact them directly to verify if any benefits are due you or the family. Likewise, Social Security notifies Medicare. But to be safe, call the customer

service number on the back of any Prescription Drug or Supplemental Insurance plans.
- Notify credit card companies and destroy cards. It is also a good idea to check credit card statements for any payments charging directly to the cards.
- Cancel club or other memberships. Check monthly bills to see exactly what needs to be cancelled. Some private club memberships are "equity" memberships and may actually have a market value. Others may provide refunds from the date of death.
- Contact airlines to see if any miles can be redeemed or transferred. Note that many airlines charge a hefty fee to transfer miles. Others offer the ability to redeem miles for gift cards or other merchandise. Look online, and then call the airline to verify your options.

Real Estate and Personal Property
- Take an inventory of personal effects and locate any additional account and loan

statements. When compiling the inventory, use a spreadsheet to list the item, its value, and who the intended recipient should be (if known). This extra step helps with the executor's final accounting.

— Contact an appraiser, as necessary, for antiques, collectibles, jewelry, and any other significantly valued items. Many items can easily be valued with a quick search online or at furniture consignment shops. However for those specialty items, an estate appraiser should be hired. Local appraisers can be found by asking your estate attorney, wealth advisor, an online search, or at www.probate.com.

— Contact the home and auto insurance company. Some insurers require notification when a covered property becomes vacant. To be sure the deceased's property does not lose coverage, notify the insurance carrier of the owners death as soon as possible. Remember to notify the auto insurance company when any vehicles are sold.

- Meet with a real estate agent to sell home. The agent should provide a market appraisal, and assist in locating contractors to help ready the home for sale.

Life Insurance

- Contact life insurance carriers to determine claim process. You'll want to determine the policy's death benefit and beneficiary designation. Most policies will list one or more primary beneficiaries and one or more contingent beneficiaries. Some policies will specify a pre-determined payout option. If none is selected, beneficiaries generally have the option of lump-sum payments or some scheduled payment stream.

Banking and Investments

- Open a bank account for the Estate. Do not close old bank accounts until all auto-payments and auto-deposits are turned off. Generally the

estate will obtain a tax identification number to be used with this account.
- Contact the bank about the IRA and the trust accounts. The bank (or brokerage firm) will change the ownership of joint accounts as appropriate and direct you to the available options for any retirement accounts. Trust accounts will be handled per the terms stated in the trust document. The trusts related to Sonya's case will be discussed in more detail below.

Taxes

- Meet with the CPA to discuss the time frame for filing the Federal Estate Tax return. The estate tax return (or Form 706) must be filed and paid within nine months of the date of death unless an extension is applied for. The IRS will generally issue an Estate Tax Closing Letter within six months after the return is filed. However, if it is selected for statistical review or examination, it could be longer. The estate may be required to file its own income tax return after its first fiscal year. Estate tax laws are complicated. The Internal Revenue Service provides useful information in Publication 950, which can be found at www.irs.gov. However for taxable estates, a competent CPA or tax attorney is strongly recommended.

- Ask the CPA about the Final Income Tax Return. Generally, if the deceased has reportable income between January 1 and the date of death, you will be required to file an income tax return for this period. The due date of this return will be April 15 (or next business day) of the year following death.
- Obtain tax identification number for the estate. Frequently, the CPA will file the appropriate IRS form for you. It can also be applied for online at www.irs.gov.

Sylvia had quite a long list of responsibilities. This was complicated because she lived out of town. Fortunately, she was able to make the time to handle her duties promptly and Robert was able to help out with some of the duties.

Final Steps

The house was not on the market for too long before selling just below the asking price. Sylvia and Robert agreed on most of the personal item distributions, only squabbling over a set of dishes. The items neither of them wanted were either sold by an estate settlement company or simply donated to local charities.

After reviewing all the documents gathered by Sylvia, the CPA determined that Sonya's total estate was just over $9 million. Approximately $170,000 was spent on final expenses, probate, and administrative fees, resulting in a taxable estate of $8.8 million. A number of factors could come into play including the date of estate valuation, prior taxable gifts, and bequests to grandchildren or charities, however Sonya's estate, though large, was quite simple.

The IRS defines the Estate Tax as "a tax on your right to transfer property at your death." Currently the IRS allows one to effectively exclude a certain amount of federal taxes owed – this is referred to as the federal estate tax exemption amount. In 2008, the year Sonya passed away, the exemption amount was $2 million and the top estate tax rate was 45% meaning the estate taxes due on her estate were over $3 million! As Ms. Sonya would say, "That's like hugging a rose bush!"

The trust established at their father's death was currently valued at $1.8 million. The terms of the trust specified that upon the death of Sonya, the full amount was to be distributed equally and outright to Sylvia and Robert Jr. and the trust be terminated. Because this trust had been created properly in Robert Sr.'s estate plan, these funds would pass directly to Sylvia and Robert with no estate taxes due. This helped to ease the shock of seeing an estate tax bill of over $3 million. The total amount distributed to Sylvia and Robert, including Sonya's estate and Robert Sr.'s trust, was nearly $7 million.

You might be wondering "How did an estate of this size, settle so smoothly?" Several factors contributed to a successful settlement process.

- **Open communication among the beneficiaries.** Oftentimes extended family and even spouses can cause riffs among the family. Clear and frequent communication is critical to allaying this issue. Sylvia was detail oriented and prepared a proper final accounting of all estate transactions occurring during the settlement process.

- **Patience by the beneficiaries.** Estate settlement does not always happen quickly. Many estate settlements can drag on for years. Frequently one or more of the beneficiaries will want "their share" now – before the estate is ready to be closed. Sometimes this can be attributed to greediness or distrust, other times it is simply ignorance of the process.
- **Patience by the Executor.** It can be tempting to close the estate as soon as possible. But it is important to not rush the process. Mistakes can easily be made if one does not take the time to properly document transactions. Additionally, it is very common for bills to continue to be presented to the estate months after death. Aside from final income tax returns, health care bills are notoriously slow. Don't distribute all the cash until you are certain all bills are paid.

- **Proper guidance by experienced team members.** It is an overwhelming experience to find yourself with the responsibility of settling a loved-one's affairs. Hiring an experienced team to guide you through the process can be invaluable.
- **Estate liquidity.** This cannot be stressed enough. The timeframe to pay the estate taxes is relatively short. Without proper wealth transfer designs, estates comprised primarily of non-marketable assets such as business interests, real estate, or other difficult to liquidate assets may be subject to estate depreciation as the assets are fire-sold.
- **Location of estate assets.** All of Sonya's assets were located in a single state. This means no secondary state tax returns or probate procedures were necessary.
- **Use of formal estate planning.** Although the estate plans implemented by Sonya and Robert Sr. were basic, and hadn't been updated for years, some planning had been done which

allowed the couple to pass nearly $4 million estate tax free.

It wasn't all roses however. The IRA beneficiary designation was 100% to Robert Jr. leading Sylvia to initially wonder if Robert had coerced their mother in giving it all to him. However, after talking to her husband about her suspicions, he reminded Sylvia that her mom and dad had paid for college for both of their children. Robert Jr. had no children, so it was really a "wash." Again, if this had been communicated by Sonya, there might not have been any suspicion.

Sylvia did have to take quite a bit of time off work to handle the affairs. The travel combined with the work was quite exhausting. Robert did what he could to help, but so much required Sylvia to either meet or sign something in-person. Additionally, they never could find the time to go through all of their parent's keepsakes, photo boxes, books, and other storage items. They are still inconveniently stored at Robert's house waiting for a time they can both sort through them.

And finally, the total estate could have been much larger. Neither Sylvia nor Robert had any real experience handling larger sums of money. Their future assets took quite a hit during the year following Sonya's death.

The estate settlement process can have its share of ups and downs. Obviously most cases involve the loss of a loved one and many are much more steeped in problems than this particular case. Do not be afraid to ask questions, even if it's the third time you've asked it. Many things need to be done in a relatively short time frame and we can speak from experience in saying it can be overwhelming. Lean on your friends and family for support and hire an experienced team to guide you. Time taken during the settlement process can save you double the time in correcting errors later.

> "There is a strange charm in the thoughts of a good legacy, or the hopes of an estate, which wondrously removes or at least alleviates the sorrow that men would otherwise feel for the death of friends."
>
> *Miguel De Cervantes*

EPILOGUE

If you have read both of our books on Sudden Wealth, you now know that sudden wealth happens more often and commonly than you might have originally thought. You will also find that sudden wealth not only brings financial challenges but emotional hurdles as well. From life events of the death of a spouse or parent, divorce, selling the family business and others, our goal in writing these books is to enlighten our readers that if and when sudden wealth occurs in your life or a love one's life, these challenges are not insurmountable. They are challenges that are to be expected. They are challenges that can be overcome. With professional help both financially and psychologically, sudden wealth can turn out to be a tool for an easier financial path and a new healthier emotional life.

Sudden Wealth... Blessing or Burden? provides a closer look at the emotional and psychological toll that a sudden wealth recipient may experience. Through the guidance and advice of our co-authors and therapists, we hope that by reading this book you will be fully prepared to handle your sudden wealth in a healthy and responsible manner.

Finally, please use this book to challenge your financial advisor to do more for you if you are in a sudden wealth situation. Financial guidance doesn't start and stop only with services that can be provided with a fee or commission. We thank you for reading and if you have questions, please contact us at www.suddenwealthhappens.com.

ABOUT THE AUTHORS

David Rust and Shane Moore are recognized wealth advisors with a combined experience of 43 years. Their passion for handling the needs of sudden wealth recipients inspired them to write the books *Sudden Wealth... It Happens and Sudden Wealth... Blessing or Burden?* They are co-founders of Quartz Financial, a comprehensive wealth management firm specializing in sudden wealth cases. Their backgrounds are deep and versatile with senior advisory positions with major banks, brokerage and insurance firms, and private banking groups.

David is a graduate of the University of Texas and holds designations, Chartered Financial Consultant, ChFC, Accredited Asset Management Specialist,

AAMS and Chartered Retirement Plans Specialist, CRPS. He holds series 7, 63 and 66 securities registrations with LPL Financial, and a Group I Life and Variable Contract Insurance License.

Shane, a graduate of Texas Tech University (MS-Finance), is a CERTIFIED FINANCIAL PLANNER professional. He holds series 7, 24, 53, 63 and 66 securities registrations with LPL Financial and a Group I Life and Variable Contract Insurance License.

Pam Monday is a licensed Marriage and Family Therapist and a Licensed Professional Counselor. She received her Ph.D in counseling Psychology from the University of Texas and has been a therapist for 30 years. She is a board approved supervisor for therapists who are beginning or expanding their counseling careers and is a frequent presenter at local, state and national conferences.

Dianne M. Arnett conducts a private practice through Talking Points Psychotherapy in Austin, Texas. She holds an undergraduate degree from the University of Texas and an MA from St. Edwards University. She is dual board certified as a licensed marriage and family therapist and a licensed Professional counselor. She teaches workshops and has served on numerous philanthropic boards in the Austin area.

Made in the USA
Lexington, KY
03 February 2015